Health Insurance Nuts and Bolts

An Introduction To Health Insurance Operations

The Health Insurance Association of America
Washington, DC 20004-1109

ISBN 1-879143-51-8

CONTENTS

FIGURES

Chapter 6

Chapter 17

FOREWORD

This book is published by the Health Insurance Association of America's Insurance Education Program. The mission of this program is to be the premier provider of self-study courses in health insurance and managed care. Included in this mission are the following goals:

- Provide tools for use by member company personnel to enhance quality and efficiency of services to the public;
- Provide a career development vehicle for employees and other health care industry professionals; and
- Further general understanding of the role and contribution of the health insurance industry to the financing, administration, and delivery of health care services.

The Insurance Education Program provides the following services:

- A comprehensive course of study in the fundamentals of health insurance, medical expense insurance, supplemental health insurance, long-term care insurance, disability income insurance, managed care, and health insurance fraud;
- Certification of educational achievement by proctored examination for all courses;
- Programs to recognize accomplishment in the industry and academic communities through course evaluation and certification, which enable participants to obtain academic or continuing education credits; and
- Development of educational, instructional, training, and informational materials related to the health insurance and health care industries.

PREFACE

Health Insurance Nuts and Bolts, together with the preceding HIAA book, *The Health Insurance Primer,* provides an introduction to group and individual health insurance. While *The Health Insurance Primer* explains basic concepts, *Health Insurance Nuts and Bolts* focuses on operations—that is, the various activities that insurance company personnel perform in order to issue, maintain, and administer health insurance policies.

This book is based on an earlier HIAA book, *Fundamentals of Health Insurance, Part B.* The topics covered are largely the same, but all information has been updated and the text has been substantially reorganized and rewritten to make concepts clearer and information easier to assimilate.

As in *The Health Insurance Primer,* greatest attention is given to the two most common forms of health insurance, medical expense insurance and disability income insurance. HIAA also offers books that focus on other health insurance coverages.

Health Insurance Nuts and Bolts, like all HIAA Insurance Education books, is accompanied by a study guide. The questions and exercises in the study guide help the reader learn the material more easily. Use of the study guides is strongly recommended to those intending to take the HIAA examinations.

This book is intended for educational purposes. Its contents are not a statement of policy. The views expressed or suggested in this and all other HIAA textbooks are those of the contributing authors or editors and are not necessarily the opinions of HIAA or of its member companies. In addition, this book is sold with the understanding that HIAA is not engaged in rendering legal, accounting, or any other professional service. If legal advice or other expert assistance is required, the services of a professional should be sought.

Terry R. Lowe HIA CLU ChFC FLMI FLHC ACS
General Reviewer and Editor

Michael G. Bell
Editor

ACKNOWLEDGMENTS

Authors

Alex Bagby ASA MAAA
Vice President and Individual Health Product Manager
American Fidelity Assurance Company

Julie L. Clopper-Smith
Coordinator, Small Group Life and Health Insurance (formerly)
The Principal Financial Group

Nancy M. Eckrich HIA FLMI AHLC AIRC ACS
Vice President, Law Department
Trustmark Insurance Company

Donald W. Kress
Vice President, Legislative and Industry Affairs (formerly)
Healthsource Provident Administrators, Inc.

Terry R. Lowe HIA CLU ChFC FLMI FLHC ACS
Superintendent, Life/Health Claims
State Farm Insurance

Martin Rosenbaum
Senior Vice President, Employee Benefits
Great West Life and Annuity

Reviewers

Mary Bailey PhD RN
Professor of Nursing and International Health
Madonna University

Robyn S. Crosson HIA FLMI
Project Lead/Business Analyst, Department of Pricing and Decision Support
Anthem, Inc.

Michelle Doherty
Vice President, Compliance and Product Filing
Federal Home Life Insurance Company

Karleen A. Dunkhas
Information Analyst
Principal Life Insurance Company

David J. Galiardo HIA
Manager, Group Benefit Operations
Alta Health and Life Insurance Company

Kelli Garvanian HIA CFE
Director, Special Investigation Unit
Trustmark Insurance Company

Susanne Lanza
Director of Managed Care Policy
Health Insurance Association of America

Deirdre A. McKenna JD
Associate Director of Insurance Education
Health Insurance Association of America

Marianne Miller
Director of Federal Regulatory Affairs and Policy Development
Health Insurance Association of America

Lillian M. Simms PhD RN FAAN
Associate Professor of Nursing Emeritus
University of Michigan School of Nursing

Patricia A. Weitzman HIA FLMI ALHC ACS AIRC
Assistant Vice President, Policy Services
Trustmark Insurance Company

Thomas Wildsmith HIA MHP FSA MAAA CLU ChFC FLMI
Policy Research Actuary
Health Insurance Association of America

General Reviewer and Editor

Terry R. Lowe HIA CLU ChFC FLMI FLHC ACS
Superintendent, Life/Health Claims
State Farm Insurance

Editor

Michael G. Bell
Assistant Director of Insurance Education
Health Insurance Association of America

ABOUT THE AUTHORS

Alex Bagby is currently an officer and manager for American Fidelity Assurance Company. As Vice President and Individual Health Product Manager, his numerous responsibilities include the design, development, and compliance of the company's portfolio of individual health policies. Bagby's background includes a degree in statistical mathematics, and he is affiliated with several professional actuarial associations.

Julie L. Clopper-Smith oversaw several underwriting and administrative teams at The Principal Financial Group, where she worked as Coordinator of Small Group Life and Health Insurance. Before beginning her career in the insurance industry, Clopper-Smith taught mathematics and computer science.

Nancy M. Eckrich is a vice president of Trustmark Insurance Company. She currently heads the Compliance Department of Trustmark's Law Department. Previously, she had responsibility for individual major medical and disability claims. Eckrich has been an active participant of the Chicago Claim Association and the Midwest Claim Conference, and she is a former General Chairperson of the Midwest Claim Conference.

Donald W. Kress has years of experience as an insurance underwriter and manager in group financial underwriting on a national level. He was formerly Vice President of Legislative and Industry Affairs for Healthsource Provident Administrators, Inc., where he managed federal and state compliance activities. Kress has also served as Chair of the Health Insurance Association of America's Insurance Education Committee.

Terry R. Lowe has enjoyed a 27-year career in the health insurance industry, with a concentration in life and individual health insurance claims. He is Superintendent of Life/Health Claims Training and Education for State Farm Insurance and is also a long-time member of the Insurance Education Committee of the Health Insurance Association of America. Lowe has served as author and editor of numerous health insurance industry publications and is an adjunct professor of insurance and business courses. He has a BS in business administration and an MBA from Illinois State University.

Martin Rosenbaum has spent 26 years in the employee benefits division of the insurance industry. As Senior Vice President of Employee Benefits for Great West Life and Annuity, he is responsible for product development in group life, health, disability, and managed care. Other responsibilities include pricing and financial reporting. Rosenbaum is a fellow of the Society of Actuaries.

1 THE ADMINISTRATION OF GROUP HEALTH INSURANCE PLANS

- *Insurer Administration and Policyholder Administration*
- *Auditing Self-Administered Plans*

- *Self-Insured Plans*
- *Third-Party Administrators (TPAs)*

Introduction

Health insurance protects people from financial loss due to an accident or illness. Providing this protection is a complex activity, involving many people and a great variety of functions. Insurance policies must be written and implemented. Records must be maintained and updated. Premiums must be billed for and collected, and claims must be processed and paid. And all of these functions must be performed in such a way that costs are kept down and an array of laws and regulations are complied with.

This book examines all of these activities. We will begin in this first chapter with an overview of the administration of group health insurance plans. We look at group plans first because their administration includes certain elements not found in individual insurance. Specifically, while individual policies are administered solely by insurer personnel, policyholders and third-party administrators play roles in running some group plans. These roles must be understood before we can proceed to our discussion of the various operations involved in administering all health insurance policies, group and individual.

Some of the operations discussed in this book are usually performed in the same way or very similarly in different insurance companies. Others are handled differently from company to company, because of differences in company size, products, and organizational structure. This book is an introductory text that seeks to give the reader a basic understanding of how health insurance operates by presenting the most common ways of doing things in the industry. But it should be kept in mind that the actual practice of any company may vary.

Insurer Administration and Policyholder Administration

As noted above, individual health insurance policies are administered by the insurance company. This means that while individual policyholders do such things as pay premiums, submit claims, and provide information, insurer personnel do the work necessary to make the policy function. Some group health insurance plans operate in the same way—insurer personnel take responsibility for the administration of the plan. But in other group plans, it is the policyholder (typically an employer purchasing coverage for its employees) that handles most of the administrative work. If the insurer handles most of the administrative functions of a plan, the plan is **insurer-administered**. If the policyholder handles most functions, the plan is **self-administered**.

In self-administration (sometimes called **self-accounting**), the employer (the policyholder) normally takes responsibility for the following activities:

- enrolling employees in the plan;
- maintaining a record for each insured employee; and
- preparing premium statements (calculating and reporting the amount of premium due to the insurer each month, which varies according to the current number of insured employees).

In some cases, the employer also administers claims or verifies employees' eligibility for benefits when claims are submitted.

In insurer administration, the insurance company performs these functions. The employer's participation is for the most part limited to submitting various reports and forms to the insurer.

If the employer handles all of the areas listed above, including claims, the insurer does not maintain its own records on individual employees. It keeps a record only of the total number of covered employees, and it obtains this information from the employer as needed.

In self-administered plans, although the employer bears primary responsibility in the areas listed above, the insurer does provide assistance. The insurer trains the employer's personnel when the plan first goes into effect, and it provides an **administration manual** that explains how the plan operates. And if unusual circumstances arise that are not covered by standard procedures, the employer can call on the insurer for guidance or handling of the situation.

Of course, since a self-administering employer relieves the insurer of most of the expense of administering the plan, the insurer charges the employer lower premiums or compensates it in some other way.

Insurer Administration or Self-Administration?

Whether a group health insurance plan is insurer-administered or self-administered depends largely on two factors:

- Is the employer capable of administering the plan? Is the business's staff large enough and does it have the necessary expertise in insurance matters? In general, larger employers are more likely to have this capability, and so self-administration is more common for large groups.
- Does the employer prefer to reduce its premiums in exchange for relieving the insurer of administrative work? Or does the employer prefer to pay the insurer more rather than take on these responsibilities?

Most insurers have some self-administered plans. A few administer all their plans themselves.

Auditing Self-Administered Plans

When an employer administers a group health insurance plan, how does the insurer know that the plan is functioning properly? And how can the insurer be sure that it is receiving the correct amount of premium and paying only those claims it is liable for? Insurers address this problem principally by means of auditing. There are two kinds of audit, external and internal.

The External Audit

An external audit takes place at the employer's facilities. (It is called external because it is done outside the insurer's offices.) An external audit is a formal process and is performed by a trained auditor. The audit addresses two main questions:

- Are the employer's records accurate?
- Is the employer correctly following administrative procedures?

In a typical external audit, the auditor might:

- examine employee enrollment cards to make sure they are being completed properly;
- count the enrollment cards to confirm the number of insured employees reported by the employer in the latest premium statement;
- review records to verify that insured employees are eligible for coverage; and
- make spot checks to determine if any claims were paid to employees who were not in fact covered by the policy.

The Internal Audit

An internal audit takes place in the insurer's own offices and is more limited and informal. It simply entails insurer personnel reviewing premium statements submitted by the employer. If they find an error, they contact the employer, find out how and why the error was made, explain proper procedure if necessary, and make sure the error is corrected.

Both external and internal audits serve two purposes: First, of course, they lead to the discovery and correction of errors and sometimes even fraud. But they also educate employer personnel on proper procedure so that fewer mistakes are made in the future. For this reason, an important part of any audit is the review of procedures with the employer's staff.

To Audit or Not to Audit?

Some insurers choose not to audit self-administered plans. It is their judgment that if procedures were adequately explained and implemented when the plan began operating, and if there have not been many obvious problems with the plan since, the plan is very likely functioning properly and an audit will discover few errors— so few that the cost of the audit will be greater than any gains that result from it. Other insurers feel that a definite need exists to audit self-administered plans and that the cost of auditing is exceeded by the resulting savings.

Another factor in the decision whether to audit is the position of state insurance department examiners. In recent years, state examiners have been subjecting self-administered plans to greater scrutiny and have asked insurers who do not audit to do so in order to protect the interests of those covered by the plan.

Self-Insured Plans

We have seen that, under the arrangement known as self-administration, some employers take on the responsibility of administering the group health insurance policies they purchase from insurers for their employees. Other employers go a step further. They not only administer their health plans, but they themselves provide the coverage and assume the financial risk. That is, instead of obtaining coverage from an insurance company, they establish their own health insurance programs for their employees and pay claims out of their own funds. These programs are known as **self-insured plans**. (Plans for which an insurer provides all coverage are sometimes called **fully insured plans** to distinguish them from self-insured plans.)

If an employer provides all of its own coverage and administers its own plan, there is, of course, no involvement by insurance companies. But, in fact, insurers sometimes do work with self-insured plans. They provide coverage to partially self-insured plans, and they provide administrative services to fully self-insured plans, acting as third-party administrators.

In a **partially self-insured plan**, the employer assumes most of the risk of paying health care benefits to its employees, but it buys some coverage from an insurer to protect itself from unusually high levels of claims. The most common form of partial self-insurance is the **minimum premium plan (MPP)**. Under this arrangement, the employer pays for its employees' normal level of claims, but if claims rise above that level, the insurer pays the excess.

Third-Party Administrators (TPAs)

Some employers want to provide their own coverage but do not have the staff or expertise needed to administer that coverage. Such an employer can establish a self-insured plan and hire a third-party administrator (TPA) to run it. A TPA is a firm that administers an insurance plan but is neither an insurer providing the coverage of the plan nor the employer purchasing the coverage (hence "third-party").

Insurance companies often act as TPAs. (Although, by definition, the TPA of a plan cannot be an insurer providing the coverage of *that particular plan*, this does not mean that it cannot be an insurer.) Insurance companies of course have extensive knowledge and experience in the administration of insurance plans and so are ideally suited for this role. Some insurers have even created separate organizational units that specialize in third-party administration.

TPAs not only administer self-insured plans; they sometimes administer fully insured plans (plans with insurer-provided coverage) as well. This occurs when an insurer provides group coverage, but neither the insurer nor the employer wants the responsibility of administering that coverage. A TPA is hired to perform this function and may, of course, be a second insurance company.

There are two principal TPA arrangements:

- **Administrative services only (ASO),** in which the TPA handles all administrative functions; and
- **Claim services only (CSO),** in which the TPA handles only claims.

Why is the first of these referred to as administrative services *only?* This term is used to distinguish this arrangement from a fully insured plan (for which an insurer provides coverage). In an ASO arrangement, the TPA (an insurer or other business) handles all administrative functions but does not provide coverage, hence the name "administrative services only."

This distinction is important for legal reasons. In an ASO arrangement in which the TPA is an insurer, the employer is not buying coverage from the insurer but rather simply paying the insurer for administrative services. Therefore, there is no insurance contract, and the arrangement between the two parties is not required to meet the standards of state insurance departments. However, it may have to meet other requirements, such as those of the Employee Retirement Income Security Act (ERISA).

Summary

In group health insurance, the insurer and the policyholder (the employer) can take a variety of roles:

- In a fully insured, insurer-administered plan, the insurer both provides coverage and administers the plan.
- In a fully insured, self-administered plan, the insurer provides coverage but the employer administers the plan.
- In a self-insured plan with no third-party administrator, the employer both provides its own coverage and administers the plan.
- In a self-insured plan with a third-party administrator, the employer provides its own coverage but an insurer or other firm administers the plan.
- Finally, in a partially self-insured plan, the employer and the insurer both provide coverage, and the employer may administer the plan itself or hire a third-party administrator.

2 THE ISSUANCE AND INSTALLATION OF POLICIES

- **Preissuance Activities for Group Policies**
- **Issuance Activities for Group Policies**
- **Installation**
- **Preissuance and Issuance of Individual Policies**

Introduction

Our examination of the various activities involved in administering a health insurance policy begins with the processes by which a policy is initiated and put into effect: issuance and installation.

The term "issuance" is used in two ways in the insurance industry. Narrowly defined, it is the act whereby an insurance company, having accepted an application for insurance and prepared a policy to provide the requested coverage, officially offers (or issues) that policy to the applicant. More broadly, issuance refers to all the various administrative activities that take place in an insurance company when a new policy is offered.

The term "installation" also refers to administrative tasks related to a new policy. But whereas issuance activities occur within an insurance company, installation is what happens in a business that is purchasing a group policy for its employees. Specifically, the business must establish procedures for record keeping, billing, submission of claims, and other functions. The business and the insurer work together to set up and put into practice these procedures.

Preissuance Activities for Group Policies

Before a group policy can be issued to an employer, the employer must complete and submit an application, pay a deposit, and provisionally enroll its employees in the policy. The tasks of insurer personnel at this stage are referred to as preissuance activities.

The Application and the Deposit

The insurer's group representative must obtain the application and the deposit from the employer. The representative verifies that the application is complete and signed, and she usually also completes a worksheet on the application with additional information needed for the underwriting and implementation of the policy.

The Enrollment of Employees

Many group plans are contributory—employees who participate pay part of the premium, and so all employees have the option of enrolling or not. For these plans, minimum enrollment requirements must be met—that is, a minimal number or percentage of employees must enroll for the policy to be issued. So that it can be determined whether this condition is satisfied, provisional enrollment of employees must take place as part of the application process. Insurer personnel are involved in enrollment in various ways.

Insurer personnel first prepare announcement literature for employees. This literature describes the proposed plan in simple, non-technical language, and includes the following information:

- the benefits of the plan;
- the requirements for eligibility for participation in the plan;
- the amount of the employee contribution to premium; and
- the proposed date on which the plan will go into effect.

Announcement literature also encourages all eligible employees to enroll.

Announcement literature is distributed to employees by employer personnel. Some employers also hold employee meetings in which the plan is presented and questions answered, and the insurer's group representative usually participates in these meetings.

To enroll in the plan, an employee must fill out, sign, and submit an enrollment form. The information on the form includes the employee's name, date of birth, sex, and occupation, as well as information on her dependents. Depending on the type of coverage, it may also include information on annual earnings. Enrollment forms serve several purposes:

- They are the official record of how many employees have enrolled and so are the basis on which it is determined whether minimum enrollment requirements have been met.
- They provide information necessary for underwriting.
- They provide information necessary for issuing certificates of coverage, for record keeping, and for other administrative tasks.

- They record employee choices, such as whether the employee wants dependent coverage or which coverage options the employee selects.
- They include employees' signed statements authorizing the employer to deduct their contributions to premiums from their wages.

If an employee chooses not to enroll, most insurers require him to sign a waiver stating that he was given the opportunity to participate but declined.

When all enrollment forms and waivers have been submitted, the insurer's group representative examines them for completeness and accuracy. She then submits the application, deposit, and enrollment forms to the insurer's home office. At this point, the issuance process begins.

Issuance Activities for Group Policies

Underwriting

The application and enrollment forms are passed to the insurer's underwriting department. This department first reviews the documents for completeness and requests any missing information from the group representative. Then the application is submitted to the underwriting process to determine whether the insurer will offer coverage to the group and on what terms. (For more information on group underwriting, see Chapter 15 of *The Health Insurance Primer.*)

The Case Summary Record

If underwriting results in the insurer offering coverage to the applying employer, insurer personnel usually prepare a case summary record (also known as an abstract, policy abstract, history card, specification sheet, or digest). This document consolidates all the information about the case that will be needed for the remaining issuance tasks (such as preparing the master policy and the employees' certificates), as well as for the administration of the plan once it goes into effect.

The Master Policy

The master policy is the legal document that establishes the agreement between the insurer and the policyholder. It states that the insurer will provide coverage in return for premiums and sets forth the terms of the agreement, including who is eligible for benefits, under what circumstances benefits will be paid, the amount of benefits, and so forth.

Most insurers have a generic model policy that is used in drawing up master policies. The model policy serves as a guide, but the provisions and wording of each master policy are tailored to the specifics of each case, as found in the case summary record. Changes may also need to be made to ensure that the master policy meets the regulatory requirements of the state in which it will be in effect.

Certificates of Insurance

Insurers usually give each insured employee a certificate of insurance. These certificates do not constitute a legal contract between the insurer and the employee. (The contract exists between the insurer and the employer and is embodied in the master policy.) Rather, certificates serve an informational purpose, outlining the benefit provisions of the master policy and the other provisions that apply to the insureds. As with master policies, insurers usually use a model certificate as a guide and develop different certificate language according to the specifics of each case.

There are two common certificate formats:

- The **master policy format**—the certificate resembles a master policy in size, style, and terminology.
- The **certificate-booklet format**—the certificate is contained in a booklet that explains the plan, using less formal terminology than a master policy.

Many insurance companies have switched to the certificate-booklet format.

Identification Cards

Most insurers distribute identification cards to insured employees, although no statute requires this. Identification cards serve as evidence of coverage that can be presented to health care providers. They also typically provide information on how to contact the insurer's customer service unit.

Other Administrative Tasks

- The billing department prepares the statement for a group's first premium.
- Forms needed to administer the plan are prepared.
- An administrative manual is prepared. As explained in Chapter One, this document explains to the employer's personnel how the health insurance plan works, what administrative tasks they will be responsible for, and how those tasks must be done.

Issuance

When insurer personnel have completed all of the above tasks, the insurer issues the policy. The insurer's group representative usually meets with the employer to deliver the master policy.

Installation

After an insurer has issued a group health insurance policy, the employer must establish the administrative procedures and structures necessary for the health insurance plan to begin operating. This process is known as installation. Insurer personnel assist the employer in installation.

Installation begins with a meeting of the insurer's group representative and the employer's **plan administrator** (the member of the employer's staff who is given the responsibility of managing the plan). In this meeting, the group representative and the plan administrator work together in the following areas:

- **The policy.** The representative reviews with the administrator the provisions of the policy that pertain to administration.
- **The administrative manual.** The representative gives the administrator the administrative manual and reviews it with her.
- **Forms and other administrative materials.** The representative explains the purpose of each administrative form and how to complete it. (This is necessary because, except for claim forms, there is little standardization among insurance companies in the design or use of administrative forms. Each company's forms reflect that company's particular organizational system.)
- **Record keeping.** The representative and the administrator set up a system for maintaining insurance records for all covered employees.
- **Claims.** The representative explains claim forms and acquaints the administrator with the deadlines and other requirements for filing claims.
- **Certificates of insurance.** The representative delivers the certificates of insurance. The representative and the administrator check the certificates for accuracy and make arrangements for their distribution to employees.

Following this initial meeting, the group representative continues to work with the plan administrator until the plan is fully operational.

Agents and Brokers

We have seen that the insurer's group representative is responsible for many tasks in the preissuance, issuance, and installation processes. In some cases, some of these tasks are instead handled by an agent or broker representing the insurer. This is most common for small groups.

Preissuance and Issuance of Individual Policies

There are obvious differences between the issuance of individual policies and that of group policies. For individual policies, there is, of course, no enrollment of employees, no establishment of employer procedures, etc. But the purpose of the issuance process is fundamentally the same for both kinds of policies, and many of the activities are similar.

Preissuance activities for individual insurance, as for group insurance, include collecting the deposit, assisting the prospective policyholder in completing the application, reviewing the application for completeness and accuracy, and submitting the application and the deposit to the home office. In individual insurance, these tasks are usually handled by an agent or broker representing the insurer.

Issuance activities are also similar to those of group policies—they include underwriting, drafting the policy, and setting up records. In one important respect, however, the issuance of individual policies is different. While one group policy covers many insureds, each person buying individual coverage must have a separate policy. As a result, in the individual insurance field, an enormous number of policies are issued. Moreover, although standard policies can be used for many people, very often policies must be individually drafted in order to address the different risks of different individuals, their varying coverage needs and requests, and the regulations of their states of residence. This results in a complex situation involving large numbers of distinct policies that does not exist in group insurance.

There is, of course, no installation of individual policies. There is no need to set up administrative procedures, as all administrative tasks are handled by the insurer and it already has structures in place to handle individual billing, claims, record keeping, etc.

Summary

Insurance company personnel work with and assist employers and individuals applying for insurance coverage. If an application is accepted, insurer personnel must perform a number of tasks related to the issuance of the policy. For all policies, this includes underwriting and drafting the policy. For group plans, certificates of insurance and identification cards must also be prepared. After issuance, group plans require a further step known as installation, in which insurer and employer personnel work together to set up the employer's administrative procedures and structures.

3 POLICY RENEWAL AND CHANGES

- *Renewal or Nonrenewal?*
- *Changes in Coverage*
- *The Renewal Process*
- *Implementing Changes in Coverage*
- *Changes in Group Plan Enrollment*
- *Changes in Insureds in Individual Policies*

Introduction

In the previous chapter we looked at how health insurance policies are initiated and put into effect. Once a policy is issued, it is in effect for a stipulated period of time, called the **term of the policy**. In addition, most health insurance policies may be renewed—that is, after the original term expires the policy may be continued. Typically, policies are renewed for a year and may be renewed each year indefinitely.

Changes are often made in the coverage provided by a policy. Benefit provisions may need to be modified to meet the changing needs of the policyholder or to address changes in risk to the insurer. Premiums may have to be increased to cover rising health care costs. Changes in coverage are most commonly (although not always) made at renewal, and so we will examine these changes and the renewal process together in this chapter.

Changes are also made in the persons covered by a policy. These changes occur continuously, not just at renewal, and so will be discussed separately at the end of the chapter.

Renewal or Nonrenewal?

In principle, when the term of a policy comes to an end, the policy is renewed if both the insurer and the policyholder agree to do so. But in fact, insurers do not usually have the right to decline to renew a health insurance policy.

Medical expense insurance is governed in this regard by the Health Insurance Portability and Accountability Act of 1996 (HIPAA). HIPAA requires insurers to renew group and individual medical expense policies except in a few specified circumstances, such as nonpayment of premiums or (for group plans) failure to maintain minimum enrollment requirements.

For some other types of health insurance, regulations may not forbid an insurer from nonrenewing a policy. However, many individual health insurance policies have renewal provisions that permit insurers to nonrenew only under certain limited circumstances. (For more information on renewal provisions, see Chapter 10 of *The Health Insurance Primer.*)

Even when insurers are free to nonrenew, they tend not to do so. Some companies nonrenew only under specific circumstances, such as the following:

- The insured has engaged in fraud. (For example, he has submitted a false claim.)
- The insured is considered a **moral hazard**. (That is, he is known to engage in dishonest or dangerous behavior.)
- The insured is overinsured. (That is, he is covered by more than one policy for the same expenses.)
- The insurer is nonrenewing an entire class of policies. (For example, an insurer may decide to get out of the disability income insurance field and so discontinues all disability policies as they come up for renewal.)

Changes in Coverage

Thus, insurers seldom nonrenew and often are not permitted to do so. What then does an insurer do if it is losing money or fears it may lose money on a policy? Usually the insurer proposes an increase in premiums or a change in coverage as a condition of renewal. For example:

- If rising health care costs are making premiums insufficient to cover claims, the insurer may propose raising premiums, increasing deductibles or coinsurance, or reducing benefits.

- If an insurer is devoting considerable time and resources to the administration of many small claims for a group or individual, it may propose increasing deductibles or elimination periods as a way of eliminating these claims.
- If an individual policyholder has adopted a more hazardous profession, the insurer may propose increasing premiums or adding an exclusion.

Generally, when an insurer proposes changes as a condition of renewal, the policyholder can either accept the changes or not renew the policy. However, in some cases, regulations or the renewal provisions of the policy limit the changes that the insurer can propose.

Changes are also made at the request of the policyholder. A policyholder may want more or less coverage or different coverage. For example:

- An individual policyholder who was formerly single but now has a family may want expanded coverage to meet her greater responsibilities.
- An individual policyholder whose salary has increased may want higher disability income benefits to cover his larger potential loss of income.
- Both group and individual policyholders may want to reduce benefits or increase deductibles or coinsurance as a way of keeping premiums down.

Insurers usually make the changes requested by policyholders whenever possible. They do this in an effort to meet the changing needs and preferences of their customers and keep their business.

Increases and Decreases in Coverage

Changes in insurance policies can be classified as either increases or decreases in coverage. Any change in a policy that increases the amount of money the insurance company is likely to have to pay in benefits is an increase in coverage. This includes adding a new benefit or increasing the amount of an existing benefit. It also includes decreasing the portion of covered expenses that insureds pay (such as deductibles or coinsurance). Conversely, any change in a policy that will likely reduce the amount the insurer will pay in benefits is a decrease in coverage. This includes eliminating an existing benefit, reducing the amount of a benefit, or increasing deductibles or coinsurance.

Since an increase in coverage leads to higher benefit payments by the insurer, coverage increases must usually be accompanied by premium increases. A decrease in coverage can make possible a decrease in premiums, or at least reduce the amount of an increase made necessary by rising health care costs.

Typically, a policyholder requests an increase in coverage because he wants more benefits and is willing and able to pay more. A decrease in coverage often occurs when an insurer, to cover rising health care costs, must either raise premiums or decrease coverage, and the policyholder chooses to keep premium rates down.

In recent years, for example, many employers and individual policyholders have held down premium increases by agreeing to higher deductibles.

The Renewal Process

Renewal Underwriting

Just as underwriting is part of the process of initially issuing a policy, it is also part of the renewal process. And renewal underwriting is much like initial underwriting—information is analyzed to determine on what terms the insurer should offer continued coverage. However, renewal underwriting does differ from initial underwriting in three ways:

- Underwriters must look for and take into account any changes in the circumstances of the policyholder or insureds since the policy was last underwritten (either at issuance or at the last renewal). For group plans, changes in the financial status of the employer, the size of the group, the characteristics of the group (such as age or gender composition), or the proportion of employees who participate in the plan can be significant. For individual policies, underwriters must consider any change in the policyholder's age, occupation, or income.
- Any problems connected with the policy must be addressed. For example, if the insurer's administrative costs have been driven up by many small claims, an increase in deductibles or elimination periods may be necessary.
- If the policyholder is requesting changes in coverage, the impact of these changes must be examined. Any additional benefits or increases in existing benefits must be analyzed to determine the probable increase in claim costs.

Collecting Information for Renewal Underwriting

Before renewal underwriting can occur, insurer administrative personnel must obtain certain information. The information needed and the work involved in compiling it varies according to the type of policy and how it is administered.

- For insurer-administered group plans, insurer personnel have most of the information they need but may have to obtain certain facts regarding individual insureds from the employer. (For example, in renewing disability income coverage, the insurer may need to know an employee's current earnings.)
- In self-administered plans, the insurer does not maintain any records on individual insureds and must obtain basic information (such as the age, sex, and earnings of individuals) from the employer.
- For individual policies, the insurer's records contain most needed facts, but some information must be requested from the policyholder. A change in the

policyholder's occupation, for example, would not be found in the insurer's records.

If an individual policyholder requests an increase in coverage at renewal, she may have to submit a new application with an updated medical history. If a decrease in coverage is requested, this is normally granted automatically without underwriting, and so no additional information is needed.

The Renewal Decision and Notice

When all necessary information has been collected, it is passed to the underwriting department. Underwriters analyze the information and make a recommendation, and the insurer makes a decision. This decision may be to nonrenew, although, as noted above, this is rare and not always permissible. Other possible decisions are renewal with no change and renewal with a change. Changes can be in premium only, in coverage only, or in both premium and coverage. Sometimes an insurer will offer two alternatives, often one with no change in coverage but an increase in premium and another with a decrease in coverage and no increase in premium (or a smaller increase).

Once the renewal decision is made, the insurer must notify the policyholder. Most states require that this be done in writing at least 30 days before the decision is to go into effect. If the insurer proposes changes in premiums or coverage, the written communication states that the policy will terminate unless the policyholder agrees to these changes. If the insurer offers alternatives, the policyholder must choose one of these or the policy will terminate. Accompanying the insurer's notice is an agreement that must be signed by the policyholder to signify acceptance.

A copy of the renewal notice is also sent to the agent or group sales representative who works with the policyholder so that this person can answer any questions and facilitate the renewal.

Implementing Changes in Coverage

When changes are made in a health insurance policy, the administrative activities involved are similar to those related to the issuance of a new policy.

For both group and individual policies, any changes must be incorporated into the master policy. Usually a rider (amendment) is added to the existing master policy, although in a few cases of very substantial changes a new master policy must be issued. If a new coverage is being added, a rider can sometimes be added and in other cases a separate policy must be issued. (Insurers prefer a rider, as it is cheaper and less complicated to administer one policy than two.)

For group policies, these additional tasks may have to be performed:

- If additional employees are made eligible for coverage (as when the plan is extended to a new class of employees or to a subsidiary company), enrollment is necessary.
- If employees already enrolled in the plan receive a new coverage (as when dental benefits are added to a plan), they must be enrolled in the new coverage.
- For any enrollments, announcement literature must be prepared and distributed.
- In some cases, new certificates of insurance may have to be issued. In other cases, riders to the existing certificates are sufficient.
- The administrative manual, various forms, and other administrative materials may need to be revised or replaced.
- If premium rates are changed, new premium statements will have to be prepared.
- The insurer's group representative or the agent working with the group may need to review the changes and go over new procedures and forms with the plan administrator.

Changes in Group Plan Enrollment

As noted in the introduction to this chapter, while changes in the coverage provided by a policy are most often made at renewal, changes in the persons insured by the policy occur continuously. In this section, we will look at how these changes arise in group plans and how they are processed.

New Employees

Employees hired after a group plan goes into effect are normally eligible for coverage and so may be added to the group of insureds. Eligibility may begin immediately upon hiring, but more often it starts after a probationary waiting period of one to three months. If the plan is noncontributory (that is, employees do not pay a portion of the premium), employees automatically become insured when they become eligible. If the plan is contributory (employees pay part of the cost of coverage and so have the option of receiving coverage or not), employees begin receiving coverage as soon as they both become eligible and choose to participate.

When coverage is to begin for an employee, an insurance record must be created for her. The employee initiates the process by filling out an enrollment card. In an insurer-administered plan, the policyholder sends the new enrollment card to the insurer, which uses it to create the record. In a self-administered plan, the employer keeps the enrollment card and creates and maintains the record itself.

Late Entrants

If a new employee chooses to join a group plan no later than 31 days after the date she becomes eligible, under most contracts she will automatically be accepted. If she does not join at that time and decides to join later, she is considered a late entrant. A late entrant must in some cases provide evidence of insurability (health and other information proving that she is an acceptable insurance risk). In other cases, a late entrant can join without providing evidence of insurability, but she must wait until the next **open enrollment period** (a period, usually lasting a few weeks and occurring once a year, during which employees can add or change coverage). If a late entrant is accepted, she is enrolled and a record created for her as for any other employee.

Certificates for New Group Members

In the past, insurers issued certificates of insurance to all newly insured employees. Some insurers still do this, but three other approaches are now more common:

- The insurer provides the policyholder with a supply of certificates with no **validation page**. (The validation page of a certificate, also called the **face page**, names the insured and states that he has the coverage described in the certificate.) When an employee is added to the plan, the insurer completes a validation page with the employee's name and sends it to the policyholder. The policyholder attaches the validation page to a certificate and delivers it to the employee.
- As above, the policyholder keeps a supply of certificates with no validation page. When an employee joins the group, the policyholder affixes a sticker with the validation information to a certificate and delivers it to the employee.
- Employees receive no certificates with personalized validation. Instead they receive booklets that indicate that they are insured if they meet the conditions set forth in the booklet.

Terminations of Eligibility for Coverage

An employee may leave a group of insureds because she is no longer eligible for coverage. She may cease to be employed by the group policyholder, or she may remain employed by the policyholder but change jobs so that she is no longer in a class of employees covered by the plan. A group policyholder must report to the insurer the names of all those who become ineligible for coverage, along with the exact date and reason for termination of eligibility.

Employee Withdrawals

An employee may also leave a group of insureds because he voluntarily chooses to stop participating in a contributory plan. Usually an employee makes this choice by signing a statement saying that he no longer authorizes his employer to deduct premium contributions from his paycheck. Withdrawal by an employee automatically terminates coverage for the employee's dependents as well.

Changes in Dependent Coverage

Dependent coverage may begin or end for an employee. There are two reasons:

- An employee may have dependents at times and not at other times. An employee may get married, get divorced, or become widowed; she may have a child or her children may reach adulthood.
- In a contributory plan, an employee may choose to add or drop dependent coverage. Premiums and employee contributions to premiums are typically higher for dependent coverage, so an employee usually chooses it only if he needs it. For example, an employee might add dependent coverage when a spouse loses her job and her own coverage and then drop it after the spouse obtains new employment and new coverage.

In a noncontributory plan, dependent coverage exists automatically whenever an employee has a dependent. In a contributory plan, an employee begins or ends dependent coverage by signing a form that authorizes increased payroll deductions.

If an employee wants to add an additional dependent at a later date (such as a new spouse or the children of a new spouse), he may have to apply for coverage. An exception is a newly born child, which HIPAA normally requires to be accepted. However, the employee must notify the insurer of the newborn within 31 days of birth.

Changes in Insureds in Individual Policies

Changes may also occur in the persons covered by an individual policy. These changes of course have nothing to do with employment but rather are always related to the policyholder's dependents. An individual policyholder may choose to add or drop dependent coverage or may gain or lose a dependent, just like a member of a group plan and for similar reasons. However, the handling of these changes for individual policies differs from that of group plans in two ways:

- When a new dependent is added to an individual policy, a rider must sometimes be issued and attached to the policy.

- When a child is no longer eligible for dependent coverage under an individual policy because he has reached the maximum age or married, the insurer usually tries to continue coverage by selling him his own policy. Some policies include a conversion privilege requiring the insurer to provide individual coverage to the adult child if he does not have coverage through employment, marriage, or some other source.

Summary

Health insurance policies can usually be renewed after their initial term expires and regularly thereafter. Before the renewal date, insurer personnel collect information, underwriters analyze this information, and a decision on renewal is made. In principle, insurers can decide not to renew a policy, but they seldom do so and in most cases are not permitted to do so. Instead, if they are losing money on a policy or fear they might, they offer to renew on the condition that changes are made in the policy. The policyholder can accept these changes or choose not to renew the policy. The policyholder can also request changes. The work of implementing changes in coverage and changes in insureds is similar to that of issuing and installing a policy.

4 PREMIUM BILLING AND PAYMENT

Introduction

This book describes the many activities that insurance company personnel perform in order to provide people with health insurance coverage. In return for this coverage, insureds pay premiums to the insurance company. In this chapter, we look at how these premiums are paid and the work of insurer personnel in this area. This includes notifying the policyholder that payment is due and receiving and processing payments.

The Premium Statement

A premium statement is a notice by which an insurer tells a policyholder that a premium of a certain amount is due by a certain date—in other words, it is a bill for the amount of premium due.

Premium statements are necessary for group policies because, although a group policyholder knows when premiums are due (due dates are set in advance and occur at regular intervals), the policyholder may not know the amount of premium due. This is because the amount for each billing period usually depends on the number of people covered by the group policy during that period and so varies as this number changes. (The number of people covered changes as employees come and go, choose to receive coverage or give up coverage, add or drop dependent coverage, or join a different class of employee with different coverage.)

For an individual insurance policy, on the other hand, the amount of the premium is the same every time, so an individual policyholder always knows both the due date and the amount due. Therefore, a premium statement is not strictly necessary for an individual policy, and in fact an insurer generally has no contractual obligation to send one. But as a practical matter, if insurers did not send individual policyholders regular reminders in the form of premium statements, the collection of premiums would be irregular and many policies would lapse due to non-payment.

Thus, insurers normally send premium statements on a regular basis to both individual and group policyholders. The exception is self-administered group plans. For these plans, the policyholder itself calculates the amount of premium due and produces a premium statement showing this calculation, which it submits to the insurer with payment. As noted in Chapter One, most insurers periodically audit self-administered plans to ensure complete payment.

Billing Periods

In group insurance, the billing period is usually a month, although some policies have annual, semi-annual, or quarterly premiums. Individual policies have a variety of payment schedules.

Calculating the Amount of a Group Premium Payment

In individual insurance, the amount of a premium is established by agreement between the policyholder and the insurer. In group insurance, on the other hand, the policyholder and the insurer establish not a premium amount but rather a **premium rate**—that is, an amount per insured person in the group. Generally there is not one premium rate but several rates, which apply to different members of the group. Different rates are assigned according to several criteria:

- **Coverages.** Different rates generally apply to group members who receive different coverages.
- **Dependent coverage.** There is generally a different rate for group members who have coverage for their dependents and those without dependent coverage.
- **Classes.** In some plans, employees are divided into different occupational classes, each with a different rate.
- **Age bands.** In some plans, a different rate applies to different age groups, such as under 25, from 25 to 29, from 30 to 34, and so on.

How then is the amount of a group premium determined? The premium amount for any billing period is obtained by multiplying each premium rate by the number of people who were insured at that rate during the period.

Group Billing Methods

There are three ways in which a group premium statement can report and bill for the number of insureds at each rate:

- **List billing.** The premium statement lists every employee insured during the current month and the premium rate for each.
- **Exception billing.** The statement does not list all employees insured during the month, only those whose coverage status or rate has changed during the month. The statement shows the total number of employees insured at each rate at the end of the previous month and the total amount of premium for the previous month; it lists those employees who have begun or ended coverage during the current month or whose rate has changed (as when an employee changes coverage, class, or age band, or adds or drops dependent coverage); and it shows the new total of insureds at each rate and the new premium amount.
- **Level or equal installment billing.** In this approach, a premium amount is computed at the beginning of each year, based on the number of insureds charged each rate at that time. The policyholder pays this amount on each premium due date during the year. It is assumed that the number of people beginning and ending coverage and changing rate categories will balance out over the course of the year such that the total amount of premiums paid for the year will be very close to the amount that would have been paid with list or exception billing.

For smaller groups, list billing is the most common method. For larger groups, where listing every insured employee every month can be time consuming, exception billing is often used. Level billing was once common but is now rare. This is because level billing results in a reasonably accurate premium amount only if a group is very stable, and most employee groups today experience significant turnover and fluctuations in size.

Some coverages, such as disability income insurance, use other billing methods.

Changes in Mid-Billing Period

In a group plan, a person may begin or end coverage in the middle of a billing period (as when an employee is hired or terminated). What amount is the group policyholder charged for a person who received coverage for only part of a month? Most policies simplify matters in this way: they charge the full monthly amount for any individual who is covered as of the premium due date, even if she was not covered for a whole month, and they charge nothing for an individual who is not covered as of the premium due date, even if she was covered at some time during the month.

In other words, if a new employee begins coverage in the middle of the month, she will be covered on the premium due date and consequently the policyholder will have to pay full price for her. On the other hand, if an employee quits and ends coverage in the middle of the month she will not be covered on the premium due date and the policyholder will pay nothing for her, even though she was covered for half the month. This rule is acceptable to both insurers and employers because, in the long term, overpayments and underpayments balance out, and both parties benefit from the simplification of billing.

What if a member of a group plan wants to make a change in coverage in the middle of a month (for example, add an optional coverage or dependent coverage)? Or what if an individual policyholder wants to increase or decrease benefits in the middle of a billing period? Many policies prohibit this—any such changes must be effective on a premium due date. But other policies do permit changes in the middle of a billing period.

However, for the amount of the next premium to reflect such a change, the change must be implemented by the **billing date**. The billing date (also known as the **billing calculation date**) is the date on which the premium statement is prepared, and the statement is based on coverage as of this date. The billing date is usually about 10 days before the premium due date. For a change to be implemented by the billing date, it must usually be requested several days beforehand.

If a change is implemented too late for the premium amount to be changed in the next premium statement, the amount changes in the following premium statement and adjustments are made retroactively—the policyholder is charged extra or credited to compensate for the time that the change in coverage was already in effect but the premium amount had not yet been changed.

Group Billing and Payment

Traditionally, an insurer sent a premium statement to a group policyholder, the policyholder mailed its payment in the form of a check to the insurer, and the insurer deposited the check at its bank. However, alternative billing and payment methods now exist for group plans. These methods have certain advantages and are increasingly used.

Lock Boxes

Some insurers have policyholders mail premium payments to post office boxes (lock boxes). A bank has access to the lock box, and it collects payments on a daily basis and deposits them in the insurer's account. The advantage of this arrangement is that payments go directly to the insurer's bank account rather than being sent to the insurer and then to the bank. The money paid can begin earning interest immediately or be available for insurer use or investment. This approach also means that insurer administrative personnel do not have to receive, endorse, and deposit payment checks, although of course the bank must be paid for its work.

Preauthorized Checks (PACs)

Alternatively, an insurer can request that policyholders give it preauthorized checks (PACs) for payment of premiums. Each month the insurer sends the policyholder a regular premium statement, but instead of showing the amount the policyholder must remit, the statement shows the amount the insurer will draw from the policyholder's account by means of a PAC. Statements are sent from three to six days before the PAC is cashed so that the policyholder can make sure that there are sufficient funds in the account.

PACs are common with small groups. Persistency (the degree to which policyholders continue with a policy) is substantially better with the PAC approach than with the traditional method of payment (policyholder remittance of checks).

Electronic Funds Transfer (EFT)

Another method of payment is the electronic movement of money from the policyholder's account to the insurer's. This is known as electronic funds transfer (EFT). EFT may be a variation on the traditional remittance method (the policyholder makes a payment to the insurer but does so electronically instead of mailing a check), or it can be used with the PAC method (the insurer draws on the policyholder's account electronically).

Many large group policyholders are moving to the use of electronic funds transfer. By adopting EFT, they can eliminate the administrative work of issuing and mailing checks, and they can improve their cash flow by making their premium payments on the last possible day, instead of having to mail them in advance to ensure arrival by the due date.

Individual Billing and Payment

Direct Billing

In the individual insurance field, the traditional method of premium payment, whereby the policyholder mails a check to the insurer in response to a regular premium statement, is known as direct billing. Direct billing of individual policies has very high administrative costs. Unlike in group insurance, where one policy covers many insureds, in individual insurance a very large number of statements and payments must be prepared and received. In addition, when policyholders must mail in their payments, the incidence of nonpayment and lapses of policies for nonpayment is high. Insurers have taken a number of approaches in addressing these problems.

Reduced Frequency of Payment

One approach is decreasing the frequency of payment. Premiums for individual policies may be monthly, quarterly, semi-annual, or annual, and obviously the more frequent the payment, the greater the costs of billing and collection. Some insurers only offer less frequent payment schedules. Other insurers give policyholders a choice of schedules, but charge more for more frequent schedules both to cover their higher costs and to discourage their use.

Lock Boxes and Automatic Bank Payments

Another approach to the problem is adopting some of the alternative payment methods used in group insurance. Premium payments can be sent to a lock box and collected directly by the insurer's bank. Preauthorized checks or electronic funds transfer can also be used—in individual insurance these two methods are together referred to as automatic bank payments.

These payment methods result in the same reduction in administrative costs and improvement in cash flow as in group insurance. In addition, automatic bank payments have a further advantage. When automatic bank payments are made for individual policies, the insurer does not send premium statements. Instead, the policyholder's bank statement serves as her confirmation that the premium was paid. As the number of premium statements in individual insurance is very large, the savings are considerable.

Credit Card Payment

Premium payments can also be charged to the policyholder's credit card. As in automatic bank payments, administrative costs are reduced because the insurer does not send a premium statement—the policyholder's credit card bill is his confirmation of payment. However, the insurer normally has to pay a fee to the credit card company, usually about 2 percent of the premium. For this reason, insurers have not been enthusiastic about this method of billing, but consumer demand is making it more common.

Payroll Deductions

It is, of course, the norm in group insurance plans to deduct employees' premium payments from their paychecks. But payroll deductions can also be used to collect premium payments for individual policies under **franchise plans**. In a franchise plan, an insurer sells individual policies to several employees of a business. The business deducts the premium amount from each employee's pay and passes that money on to the insurer. The insurer's costs are reduced because instead of billing and collecting from each individual policyholder, it submits one premium statement to the employer and receives one lump sum for all policyholders. (It should be clarified that franchise plans are a form of individual, not group insurance. Each insured has his own individual policy—the employer is not a party to an insurance contract but simply facilitates the payment of premiums as a service to its employees.)

The Grace Period, Termination, and Reinstatement

The Grace Period for Payment of Premiums

Regulations require all individual health insurance policies to have a grace period for the payment of premiums, and most group policies also have them. A grace period is a time during which the insurer may not terminate the policy even if the policyholder has failed to pay a premium. The grace period begins on the due date and most commonly lasts 31 days. The purpose of the grace period is to protect a policyholder with a temporary budget problem or one who simply forgets to mail the premium payment on time.

Termination and Reinstatement

If a premium remains unpaid after the grace period expires, coverage ceases to be in effect. The insurer may terminate the policy by formally notifying the policyholder that it is doing so. However, in most cases the insurer tries to persuade the policyholder to pay and continue the policy. If the policyholder does pay, the insurer will usually reinstate the policy (put it back into effect).

In some cases, insurers require individual policyholders to apply for reinstatement. The policyholder must submit an application with information on the health history of those persons insured under the policy. The reinstatement provisions of most individual policies set these rules for reinstatement applications:

- If the insurer accepts a premium payment after the end of the grace period without requiring that an application be submitted with the payment, it must reinstate the policy with no application.
- If the insurer does require an application with a late premium payment, it has 45 days after this payment to decide whether to reinstate the policy. If it does not notify the policyholder of its decision within 45 days, the policy must be reinstated.

Summary

Insurer administrative activities associated with the payment of premiums include billing and receiving and processing payments. Billing normally involves preparing premium statements and sending them to policyholders. For individual policies, preparing each statement is not difficult, but there are a great many statements. For group policies, there are a small number of statements, but for each one the number of persons insured at each premium rate must be determined and the amount of premium calculated. A number of new approaches to billing and payment have been adopted, including lock boxes, preauthorized checks (PACs), electronic funds transfer (EFT), credit card payment, and payroll deductions.

5 CLAIM ADMINISTRATION

- *Home Office Claim Departments*
- *Field Claim Offices*
- *Self-Administration*

Introduction

When a person incurs a loss covered by an insurance policy, she must submit a claim—a declaration of the loss accompanied by any necessary proof—to the insurance company. Insurer personnel examine the claim and, if it is valid, the insurer pays a benefit. Traditionally, the terms "claims," "claim administration," and "claim department" have been used in referring to the activities and personnel involved in this process. We follow this traditional usage, but it should be pointed out that more recently focus has shifted to the end product of the process and the terms "benefits," "benefits administration," and "benefits department" are increasingly used.

The chapters that follow this one discuss how claims are submitted and processed and how benefits are paid. But first, in this chapter, we look at who is responsible for claim administration and how claim operations are organized. This varies from insurer to insurer and policy to policy.

Home Office Claim Departments

Some insurers handle all claim administration in their home office, while others maintain a number of field claim offices. There are a number of advantages to the home office approach. It is usually less costly to maintain one large unit rather than several smaller ones. Also, concentrating all claim personnel in one location centralizes training and simplifies the communication of changes in procedures, making it easier to maintain consistent and correct practice. Another advantage is the proximity of all claim personnel to other insurer staff they may need to consult, such as physicians and attorneys.

Home office claim operations are usually organized in one of two ways:

- **Single department organization.** There is a single claim department for all the types of coverage the insurer offers. This department coordinates its activities with the other departments of the company, such as sales, marketing, and underwriting.
- **Product line organization.** There is a separate claim department for each type of coverage (product line). Each of these claim departments is part of a larger department that handles all activities associated with that coverage. For example, a company might be divided into departments for medical expense insurance, disability income insurance, supplemental coverages, and so forth, with each department responsible for the sales and marketing, underwriting, and claims for that coverage.

There is a trade-off in the choice between these two organizational models. In product line organization, each claim department is focused on a single kind of coverage. This allows departmental procedures and policies to be tailored to that coverage and enables departmental personnel to become more experienced in the particular needs and problems of the coverage. On the other hand, product line organization may lead to a lack of consistency in the treatment of claims for the insurer's different types of coverage.

Conversely, single department organization results in a high degree of consistency but limited specialization. It is true that in a department that deals with claims for all coverages, staff below the managerial level may specialize to some degree, but specialization is always limited by the need for staffing flexibility, which requires most personnel to be trained and experienced in handling several product lines.

Field Claim Offices

Other insurance companies maintain several field claim offices where claim administration takes place. This approach is sometimes referred to as **geographic organization**. With field claim offices, the advantages of the concentration of operations and proximity to other staff are lost, but because the field staff is closer to policyholders, more personalized service can be provided.

The number of field claim offices that an insurer maintains varies greatly, depending on the geographic distribution of its policyholders and insured population, the type of coverages it offers, and the number of field offices maintained by its competitors. The size of field claim offices and the volume of claims they process also vary greatly.

The current trend is toward concentrating all claim operations in one office, due to the savings in costs. New technologies also facilitate the centralization of claim operations.

Self-Administration

As explained in Chapter One, some group health insurance plans are self-administered—that is, they are managed not by the insurer but by the group policyholder (usually a business providing group coverage to its employees). In such plans, the employer's responsibilities may include claim administration. If this is the case, the employer receives and processes claims and pays benefits and the insurer reimburses the employer for the amounts paid.

Employer claim administration is not common. When it occurs, it most often involves short-term disability income insurance and basic medical expense insurance, which are relatively uncomplicated. Insurers rarely allow employers to administer claims for more complex coverages.

More common is **policyholder submission**. In this arrangement, the policy-holder/employer does not take full responsibility for processing claims, but it does participate in the process. It receives claims from its employees, reviews them to verify coverage, and submits them to the insurer for processing and payment. Policyholder submission is discussed in more detail in the next chapter.

Insurer Involvement in Employer Claim Administration

An employer that administers claims selects and supervises its own claim personnel; the insurer exercises no direct control over these people. However, the insurer can take measures to ensure that they process claims correctly:

- Insurer personnel usually assist in the training of employer claim personnel.
- Many insurers require that when employer personnel deal with a complicated or questionable claim, they consult with insurer claim staff.
- Insurers conduct periodic audits of the claim operations of employers to ensure that the appropriate procedures are in place and are being followed.

The three most common types of claim audits are:

- **Large amount audit.** Any claim in excess of a certain amount is referred to insurer personnel for review and approval before payment is made.
- **Random sample audit.** The employer's plan administrator sends the insurer a random sample of claim files of cases that have been closed. Insurer claim personnel review the cases to determine whether proper procedures were followed.

● **On-site audit.** A representative of the insurer visits the employer and reviews randomly selected closed and active files to determine whether proper procedures are being followed. The insurer representative can also interview the employer's personnel to determine whether they have an adequate understanding of these procedures.

Reimbursement for Claim Payments

As noted above, when an employer handles claim administration, the employer pays all claims and the insurer reimburses for the amounts paid. Reimbursement is usually done by means of the **policyholder draft (or draft book) system**.

A draft is like a check, in that both are used to draw money from an account, but there are important differences. A check must be paid whenever it is presented, so as soon as a check is written, there must be sufficient funds in the account to pay it. A draft, on the other hand, is not necessarily paid as soon as it is presented, and there do not have to be sufficient funds in an account when a draft is submitted. When a draft is made on an account, it can be accepted or denied by the holder of the account, and if it is accepted, funds are then deposited to pay it.

In the policyholder draft system, the insurer gives the employer (the group policyholder) a supply of drafts (a draft book). When the employer pays a claim, it submits a draft on the account of the insurer. The employer also sends a copy of the draft to the insurer. (Usually all drafts for each day are sent together.) Some insurers require that the claim form and associated documentation be included with the draft copies. The insurer then accepts or denies the draft. If the draft is accepted, the employer draws money from the insurer's account and uses this money to cover the cost of claims.

Summary

Claim administration may be organized in a number of different ways. An insurer may perform all operations in its home office, either in one large claim department or in separate claim departments for each product line. Alternatively, an insurer may handle claims in several field claim offices. Self-administered group plans may process their own claims. Other group plans practice policyholder submission of claims. When employers handle claims, the insurer must take measures to ensure that proper procedures are followed. These include training, consultation on difficult cases, and audits.

6 THE SUBMISSION OF CLAIMS

- **Direct Submission**
- **Self-Administered Plans and Policyholder Submission**

- **The Two Steps in Submitting a Claim**

Introduction

For an insurance company to pay benefits for a loss, it must receive a claim. A claim is a statement that a covered loss has occurred accompanied by information about the loss and sometimes proof of it. There are a number of arrangements for the submission of claims: An insured, a health care provider, or an employer may submit claims, and an insurer or employer may receive them. This chapter discusses these arrangements.

The information in this chapter and the following one applies to most health coverages. Claim administration for disability income insurance, however, differs in some significant ways and is covered separately in Chapter Eight.

Direct Submission

In some group plans, as we will see later, insureds submit their claims to the group policyholder (their employer). For most group plans, however, and of course for all individual policies, claims are submitted directly to the insurer without employer involvement. This is known as direct submission.

Traditionally, direct submission has functioned in one of these two ways:

- An insured receives health care services, fills out a claim form, and sends the form, along with any necessary information and documentation, to the insurer. If the claim is valid, the insurer pays the benefit to the insured, who then pays the health care provider if she has not already done so. Alternatively, the insurer pays the benefit directly to the provider. In some cases the insurer does this automatically, and in other cases the insured must formally request it—that is, she must **assign benefits** to the provider.

• The provider, with the authorization of the insured, fills out a claim form and submits it along with a bill on the insured's behalf. Under this arrangement, the insurer usually pays the benefit directly to the provider.

In recent years, two systems that make direct submission easier for insureds have become common: the card-only system and the claim-kit system. These approaches were created for large group plans but are now also used for smaller groups and individual policies.

The Card-Only System

The card-only system is much more common than the claim-kit system. This arrangement is a variation on provider submission of claims. The insurer provides each insured with an identification card. This card states that the cardholder has health coverage and summarizes the benefits she is entitled to. The card usually also indicates that the insurer will pay these benefits directly to the health care provider. When the insured needs health care services, she presents the card to the provider, who submits the claim and is paid by the insurer.

The Claim-Kit System

This arrangement is a combination of the card-only system and submission of claims by the insured. The insurer provides each insured with a claim kit containing an identification card like that used in the card-only system but also claim forms and instructions on how to submit a claim. For major services (such as surgery or hospitalization), the insured uses her card just as in the card-only system. But for minor services (such as a visit to a physician's office), she pays the provider out of her own pocket and submits a claim to the insurer. The insurer then reimburses the insured for any covered expense.

Self-Administered Plans and Policyholder Submission

As explained in the previous chapter, in a few self-administered group plans the group policyholder (the employer) administers claims. That is, the employer processes and pays claims and is reimbursed by the insurer. In such plans, employees do not submit claims to the insurer, but rather to the employer.

In addition, there are other group plans in which the employer does not process and pay claims but does participate in claim administration. This practice is known as policyholder submission because the group policyholder (the employer) receives claims from employees and submits them to the insurer, rather than insureds submitting claims directly to the insurer (direct submission).

Under policyholder submission, employees fill out claim forms and deliver them to the employer. The employer reviews each claim and checks its records to confirm that the employee has coverage. The employer then submits the claim to the insurer, certifying coverage. The insurer may pay benefits directly to the insured or a provider or may pay the employer, which passes the payment to the insured.

Policyholder submission requires that the employer maintain an insurance record for each covered employee, even though the employer is not administering claims. Policyholder submission is less common than direct submission, but it is practiced by some small and medium-size employers.

The Two Steps in Submitting a Claim

The Notice of Claim

The first step in making a claim is submitting the notice of claim. In a notice of claim, the insured (now the **claimant**) or a provider acting on the insured's behalf notifies the insurer that a loss covered by the policy has occurred. This action makes the insurer aware that it should begin the preliminary work of assembling a claim file and determining the status of the policy. It also serves as a request by the insured for forms needed for the second step, submitting proof of loss.

All group and individual health insurance policies contain a notice of claim provision. This typically states that notice of claim must be made in writing within 20 days after the loss or as soon thereafter as is reasonably possible.

Proof of Loss

The second step is submitting proof of loss. When a claim is being submitted by an insured, she usually provides proof of loss by answering the questions on a claim form supplied by the insurer and attaching any bills or other documentation to it. The insurer's claim form is designed to establish the facts necessary to evaluate and process a claim. Providers may also submit insurer claim forms, but hospitals and large clinics and the physicians working at them often use their own claim forms, and some providers simply submit a bill. Most insurers will accept any form or bill, provided that it contains the necessary information.

In practice, notice of claim and proof of loss are often combined. For example, if a provider does not use the insurer's form, or if an insured already has a copy of the insurer's form, neither needs to take the step of requesting one. They may simply submit a form or bill, which will serve simultaneously as both notice of claim and proof of loss. However, if this approach is taken, the form or bill must be received within the 20-day deadline for notice of claim. If the insured or provider is unable to submit proof of loss within 20 days, he must first submit notice of claim and later deliver proof of loss.

Contract provisions typically state that proof of loss must be submitted within 90 days after the loss or as soon as is reasonably possible.

Standard Claim Forms

As noted, insurers accept a variety of claim forms and bills, as long as they provide the information needed to process the claim. However, in an effort to increase uniformity and so make the claim process less complicated and easier for both health care providers and insurer personnel, standard claim forms have been developed for use by all. These forms are designed to be simple but flexible enough to be used in a wide variety of cases and suited to the needs of both insurers and providers. The most important of these forms are the following:

- **The Uniform Billing Form (UB-92; HCFA-1450)** is used by hospitals and other institutions. It provides information on the diagnosis of the insured; the treatments, services, and supplies provided; and the amounts charged. (See Figure 6.1.)
- **The Health Insurance Claim Form (HCFA-1500)** is used by physicians and other non-institutional health care providers. Like UB-92, HCFA-1500 provides information on diagnoses, treatments, services, supplies, and charges. (See Figure 6.2.)

The Uniform Billing Form has been adopted by Medicare and Medicaid and is accepted by the majority of insurers. The Health Insurance Claim Form has been approved by the American Medical Association as part of its efforts to reduce and simplify insurance paperwork for health care providers. Many states have enacted legislation mandating insurer acceptance of these forms, and others are expected to follow suit.

Summary

The submission of a claim may be done in a number of ways. The insured herself may submit the claim, or a health care provider may do so. The card-only or claim-kit system may be used to facilitate submission. Claims for individual policies are always submitted directly to the insurer; claims for most group plans are also submitted to the insurer, but in other plans they may be delivered to the employer.

FIGURE 6.1

Uniform Billing Form

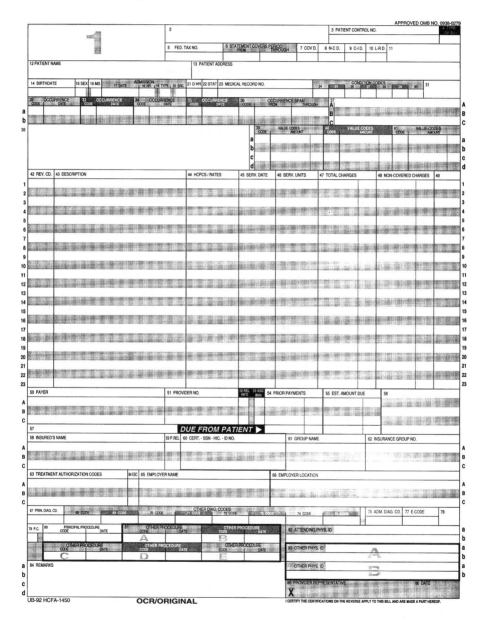

FIGURE 6.2

Health Insurance Claim Form

PLEASE
DO NOT
STAPLE
IN THIS
AREA

APPROVED OMB-0938-0008

CARRIER →

| | PICA | | **HEALTH INSURANCE CLAIM FORM** | | PICA | | |

1. MEDICARE   MEDICAID   CHAMPUS   CHAMPVA   GROUP HEALTH PLAN   FECA BLK LUNG   OTHER
(Medicare #)   (Medicaid #)   (Sponsor's SSN)   (VA File #)   (SSN or ID)   (SSN)   (ID)

1a. INSURED'S I.D. NUMBER   (FOR PROGRAM IN ITEM 1)

2. PATIENT'S NAME (Last Name, First Name, Middle Initial)

3. PATIENT'S BIRTH DATE   MM | DD | YY   SEX   M □   F □

4. INSURED'S NAME (Last Name, First Name, Middle Initial)

5. PATIENT'S ADDRESS (No., Street)

6. PATIENT RELATIONSHIP TO INSURED   Self □   Spouse □   Child □   Other □

7. INSURED'S ADDRESS (No., Street)

CITY   STATE

8. PATIENT STATUS   Single □   Married □   Other □
Employed □   Full-Time Student □   Part-Time Student □

CITY   STATE

ZIP CODE   TELEPHONE (Include Area Code) ( )

ZIP CODE   TELEPHONE (INCLUDE AREA CODE) ( )

9. OTHER INSURED'S NAME (Last Name, First Name, Middle Initial)

10. IS PATIENT'S CONDITION RELATED TO:

11. INSURED'S POLICY GROUP OR FECA NUMBER

a. OTHER INSURED'S POLICY OR GROUP NUMBER

a. EMPLOYMENT? (CURRENT OR PREVIOUS)   YES □   NO □

a. INSURED'S DATE OF BIRTH   MM | DD | YY   SEX   M □   F □

b. OTHER INSURED'S DATE OF BIRTH   MM | DD | YY   SEX   M □   F □

b. AUTO ACCIDENT?   YES □   NO □   PLACE (State)

b. EMPLOYER'S NAME OR SCHOOL NAME

c. EMPLOYER'S NAME OR SCHOOL NAME

c. OTHER ACCIDENT?   YES □   NO □

c. INSURANCE PLAN NAME OR PROGRAM NAME

d. INSURANCE PLAN NAME OR PROGRAM NAME

10d. RESERVED FOR LOCAL USE

d. IS THERE ANOTHER HEALTH BENEFIT PLAN?   YES □   NO □   *If yes*, return to and complete item 9 a-d.

READ BACK OF FORM BEFORE COMPLETING & SIGNING THIS FORM.
12. PATIENT'S OR AUTHORIZED PERSON'S SIGNATURE I authorize the release of any medical or other information necessary to process this claim. I also request payment of government benefits either to myself or to the party who accepts assignment below.

SIGNED _____   DATE _____

13. INSURED'S OR AUTHORIZED PERSON'S SIGNATURE I authorize payment of medical benefits to the undersigned physician or supplier for services described below.

SIGNED _____

14. DATE OF CURRENT: ILLNESS (First symptom) OR   INJURY (Accident) OR   PREGNANCY(LMP)   MM | DD | YY

15. IF PATIENT HAS HAD SAME OR SIMILAR ILLNESS. GIVE FIRST DATE   MM | DD | YY

16. DATES PATIENT UNABLE TO WORK IN CURRENT OCCUPATION   FROM   MM | DD | YY   TO   MM | DD | YY

17. NAME OF REFERRING PHYSICIAN OR OTHER SOURCE

17a. I.D. NUMBER OF REFERRING PHYSICIAN

18. HOSPITALIZATION DATES RELATED TO CURRENT SERVICES   FROM   MM | DD | YY   TO   MM | DD | YY

19. RESERVED FOR LOCAL USE

20. OUTSIDE LAB?   YES □   NO □ $ CHARGES

21. DIAGNOSIS OR NATURE OF ILLNESS OR INJURY. (RELATE ITEMS 1,2,3 OR 4 TO ITEM 24E BY LINE)
1. L___ . ___   3. L___ . ___
2. L___ . ___   4. L___ . ___

22. MEDICAID RESUBMISSION   CODE   ORIGINAL REF. NO.

23. PRIOR AUTHORIZATION NUMBER

24. A DATE(S) OF SERVICE						B Place of Service	C Type of Service	D PROCEDURES, SERVICES, OR SUPPLIES (Explain Unusual Circumstances) CPT/HCPCS	MODIFIER	E DIAGNOSIS CODE	F $ CHARGES	G DAYS OR UNITS	H EPSDT Family Plan	I EMG	J COB	K RESERVED FOR LOCAL USE
From MM	DD	YY	To MM	DD	YY											
1																
2																
3																
4																
5																
6																

25. FEDERAL TAX I.D. NUMBER   SSN □ EIN □

26. PATIENT'S ACCOUNT NO.

27. ACCEPT ASSIGNMENT? (For govt. claims, see back)   YES □   NO □

28. TOTAL CHARGE $

29. AMOUNT PAID $

30. BALANCE DUE $

31. SIGNATURE OF PHYSICIAN OR SUPPLIER INCLUDING DEGREES OR CREDENTIALS (I certify that the statements on the reverse apply to this bill and are made a part thereof.)

SIGNED _____   DATE _____

32. NAME AND ADDRESS OF FACILITY WHERE SERVICES WERE RENDERED (If other than home or office)

33. PHYSICIAN'S, SUPPLIER'S BILLING NAME, ADDRESS, ZIP CODE & PHONE #

PIN#   GRP#

PATIENT AND INSURED INFORMATION   PHYSICIAN OR SUPPLIER INFORMATION

(APPROVED BY AMA COUNCIL ON MEDICAL SERVICE 8/88)   *PLEASE PRINT OR TYPE*   FORM HCFA-1500 (U2) (12-90)   FORM OWCP-1500   FORM RRB-1500

Employers may process and pay claims, or they may only review claims, confirm coverage, and submit claims to the insurer for processing and payment.

Submitting a claim consists of two steps: notice of loss and proof of loss. A claim form is usually used to submit proof of loss. Claim forms are provided by insurers, but some providers use their own forms or standard forms.

7 CLAIM PROCESSING

- **Was Coverage in Effect?**
- **Is the Loss Covered?**
- **What Is the Amount of Benefit?**
- **Paying a Benefit or Denying a Claim**
- **Claim Investigations**
- **Hospital Audits**
- **Claim Administration and Customer Service**

Introduction

Once a claim has been submitted, the insurer's claim examiners and other claim personnel begin their work. They must determine whether a benefit is in fact due to the insured and, if so, what the amount of that benefit is. To make this determination, they must examine both the facts of the case and the provisions of the insured's policy. The circumstances surrounding illness and injury and their treatment may be complicated, and there is a great diversity of health insurance policies, each having a large number of provisions. Consequently, examining and processing health insurance claims is a complicated job.

However, we can simplify by saying that claim processing essentially consists of seeking the answers to three questions:

- Was the policy in effect when the insured incurred a loss?
- Is the particular loss the insured incurred covered by the policy?
- What amount of benefit does the policy pay for this loss?

Only if the answer to the first two questions is "yes" will a benefit be paid. If this is the case, the third question must be asked—that is, the amount of benefit must be determined.

Was Coverage in Effect?

The first issue that must be addressed in claim processing is **status of coverage.** It must be determined whether the claimant was in fact covered by the policy when the loss occurred. To decide this, three questions must be answered:

• When exactly did the loss occur?
• Had coverage begun at that time?
• Had coverage lapsed or ended at that time?

If a loss occurred before coverage went into effect, or after coverage ceased to be in effect, or at a time when coverage had temporarily lapsed, the insured is not entitled to benefits.

For a group plan, the issue of status of coverage must be addressed on two levels:

• When was coverage of the group in effect?
• When was coverage of the individual member of the group in effect?

Both the group policy and the coverage of the individual group member must be in effect at the time of loss or the insurer is not liable for benefits.

As noted in the previous chapter, when policyholder submission is practiced, the group policyholder is responsible for checking status of coverage before submitting a claim to the insurer.

Date of the Loss

First, the date of the loss must be established. The date on which an injury occurred is usually clear-cut. The date of the onset of some illnesses is also clearly definable. On the other hand, there are many cases in which it is difficult to say precisely when a medical condition began. Many conditions start with vague symptoms that the individual may ignore for a time before seeking medical attention. The exact dates when these symptoms first appeared may be hard for the insured to remember.

Because of this difficulty in establishing the actual date on which a medical condition began, for practical purposes the date of the onset of a condition is defined as the date when medical treatment was first sought. An exception to this rule is made if a person delayed seeking medical attention when it was clearly needed. In such a case, onset is considered to have occurred when symptoms were such that an ordinarily prudent person would have sought treatment.

Beginning of Coverage

The date on which an insured begins to be covered by an insurance policy is the **effective date of coverage**. If a loss occurs before this date, there is no coverage for that loss. The effective date of coverage is established by the policy.

- Group policies establish a specific date (such as August 14) as the effective date. This date is agreed to by the policyholder and the insurer as part of the contract.
- Individual policies usually stipulate that the effective date is the date of application, provided certain conditions are met. (Normally, the applicant must have paid the first premium; in some cases, he must have submitted a medical examination report that the insurer finds acceptable.)

End of Coverage and Lapse of Coverage

In Chapter Four, we discussed the lapse of coverage for nonpayment of premiums, the grace period for payment of premiums, and the termination and reinstatement of policies. Policy provisions relating to these matters are factors in determining whether and when coverage ended or lapsed temporarily and so whether a loss incurred at a particular time was covered by a policy.

- For both individual and group policies, during the grace period coverage remains in effect. That is, losses incurred during the grace period are covered, whether the policy is eventually reinstated or not.
- For both individual and group policies, if a policy lapses and is not reinstated, coverage does not continue after the end of the grace period. Losses incurred after the grace period ends are *not* covered.
- For group plans, if a policy lapses but is reinstated, losses incurred after the end of the grace period but before reinstatement are covered.
- For individual policies, if a policy lapses but is reinstated, losses incurred after the end of the grace period but before reinstatement *are usually not* covered. The Uniform Policy Provision Law (UPPL), which has been adopted by most states, only requires individual policies to cover injuries occurring after the date of reinstatement and illnesses beginning more than 10 days after that date. Some insurers liberalize this provision and cover illnesses that begin any time after the date of reinstatement.

Validity of the Policy

In a few cases, coverage may not be in effect because the policy itself is invalid. The reason is most often that the policyholder made material misrepresentations in the application for insurance. Misrepresentations are false statements; material misrepresentations are false statements significant enough that if the insurer had known the truth, it would not have offered coverage or would have offered it on substantially different terms. The most common instance of this is when an applicant for individual coverage does not report an existing or past medical condition.

In these cases, if the condition is such that the insurer would not have offered coverage under any circumstances, the insurer usually rescinds (annuls) the policy. If the condition is such that the insurer would have offered a policy with a special provision (such as an exclusion or a higher premium), the insurer may offer to add that provision to the policy, effective retroactively to the date of issue. If the insured rejects a retroactive revision of the policy, the insurer normally rescinds the policy.

An insurer is permitted to rescind an individual insurance policy because of misrepresentations in the application only during the first two years (three years in some states) following the issue date of the policy. This period is known as the **contestable period**. After this time, a policy may not be rescinded on these grounds.

Is the Loss Covered?

Once it has been established that the claimant's coverage was in effect at the time of the loss, claim examiners look at the claim form, bills, and other documents and ask these questions:

- What health care services or supplies is the insured making a claim for?
- Are these services and supplies covered by the benefit provisions of the insured's policy?
- Are there any other provisions of the policy that would make benefits not payable?

Health insurance policies have a wide variety of provisions. It is the job of a claim examiner to look at every expense claimed and determine whether it is in fact covered by the policy in question.

First, the claim examiner reviews the claim form, bills, and any other documents that have been submitted and puts them in order. A large claim may include many different expenses, and there may be many bills from a number of providers for a variety of services and supplies. The examiner reviews these bills to confirm that each one pertains to the person making the claim and the condition reported on the claim form.

Next, the examiner determines whether the type of expense claimed is covered by the benefit provisions of the policy. For example, if a claimant is seeking reimbursement for the expense of diagnostic X-rays, the examiner must review benefit provisions to ascertain whether they include this service.

Next, the examiner ascertains whether there are any other provisions of the policy that disallow the claimed expense. For example, a policy may have exclusions that eliminate benefits for preexisting conditions or for losses that occurred under certain circumstances. A policy may also have elimination periods that must expire before benefits are paid or benefit periods after which benefits are no longer paid. Or an overall maximum benefit provision may limit the total amount of benefits paid on the policy.

In addition, policies for most kinds of health insurance have provisions stating that benefits will be paid only for services and supplies that are medically necessary. Therefore, another part of examining a claim is identifying unnecessary services. This begins with the screening of claims for services that are not usual for the medical condition of the claim. Most insurers develop **screening guides** for this purpose. These guides contain information on the treatments and services usually provided for many medical conditions. The average length of hospital stay for each condition and the average duration of disability, if any, are also provided, usually with adjustments for the age and sex of the patient. Insurers obtain this information from recognized health care professional groups and publications, agencies of the federal government, and their own claim data.

If an examiner discovers a service that is not usual for the claimant's condition, she does not assume that it was not needed, as there are sometimes unusual circumstances that make unusual treatment necessary. But the examiner does seek more information to ascertain whether the service was necessary or not. For example, a screening guide might state what the usual number of days of hospital stay is for a patient of a certain age and sex, with a certain condition, undergoing a certain procedure. If the insured is kept in the hospital longer, the examiner would contact the hospital or physician to find out why this was done. Normally, there is a good reason, but if not, benefits for the additional days might be denied.

What Is the Amount of Benefit?

If it is determined that an expense is covered and a benefit will be paid, the amount of the benefit must be determined. In some cases, the dollar amount of a benefit is set by the policy, as with lump-sum payments or per-day hospital benefits. In other cases, the policy includes a benefit schedule that sets maximum dollar amounts for given expenses. Finally, very commonly the benefit amount for a service is the amount charged by the provider, as long as the amount charged does not exceed certain limits, known as **eligible charge limits.**

The eligible charge limit for a service is usually defined as the reasonable and customary charge for that service. (For this reason, eligible charge limits are also known as **reasonable and customary charge limits**.) The reasonable and customary charge for a service is the amount normally charged for that service or a similar service by similar health care providers in the same geographic area. Alternatively, some policies define the eligible charge limit for a service as the reasonable and customary charge or the provider's usual charge, whichever is less.

If a provider charges more than the eligible charge limit of a policy, the insurer will normally pay only the amount of the eligible charge limit. However, the examiner may contact the provider to see if there were complications or special conditions that might justify a higher than normal charge.

Each insurer establishes its own reasonable and customary charge guidelines. For every health care service, each insurer analyzes data on charges in an attempt to arrive at a number that accurately reflects what providers in the area are charging. But insurers may use different bodies of data and somewhat different methods of analysis, so as a result, reasonable and customary amounts are similar for different insurers, but they are not exactly the same.

The data that insurers analyze to calculate reasonable and customary charges comes from various sources. The **Prevailing Healthcare Charges System (PHCS)** is an important organization in this field. The PHCS collects a very large amount of data on the claims submitted to many different insurers. From this data, it derives information on the amounts charged for various health care services and publishes this information in semi-annual reports that it sends to insurers that subscribe to the service. These reports show charges by service and geographic area and include various statistical analyses. Participating insurers generally combine this information with data from their own claims to set their reasonable and customary charge amounts.

After the claim examiner has calculated the amount of a benefit based on a preset amount, a benefit schedule, or the provider's charges and eligible charge limits, she must consider two additional factors before she can determine the amount of benefit payment. She must take into account any deductibles, coinsurance, or copayments that the insured is responsible for. These must be deducted from any benefit payment unless the insured has already paid them. In addition, the examiner must find out whether another insurance policy is paying benefits for the same loss, and if so take those benefit payments into account. This is done by means of a process known as coordination of benefits (COB).

Coordination of Benefits (COB)

Sometimes a single loss is covered by two different insurance policies. This phenomenon is known as **overinsurance.** How might overinsurance occur in the health insurance field?

- A person may have two individual health insurance policies with overlapping coverage.

- A person covered by her employer's group health plan may also have an individual policy.
- A person covered by an employer's group plan may also be covered by a second group plan through a second employer or a professional association.
- A husband and wife may both have employer-sponsored group health coverage that includes dependent coverage, so that both of them, as well as any dependent children, are covered by both plans.

Overinsurance presents an obvious problem: Most kinds of health insurance are intended to help insureds pay for medical expenses, but when an insured is overinsured, she can make two claims for the same loss and so receive much more in benefits than she has actually incurred in expenses. This is not the purpose of insurance. There is also a less obvious problem—because overinsurance leads to claim payments that are higher than needed to meet the legitimate needs of insureds, and because insurers must charge enough in premiums to cover the cost of claim payments, overinsurance leads to unnecessarily high premiums. This problem is compounded because an overinsured person can actually make money by receiving double benefits, and so overinsurance gives such people financial incentives to use health care services even when they do not need them. This further drives up claim payments and premiums.

In response to these problems, the insurance industry has developed policy provisions that allow for coordination of benefits (COB). COB is a process whereby two or more insurance companies that insure the same person for the same losses coordinate their payments of benefits so that they do not overlap and so that the amount of benefits received by the insured is never greater than the amount of expenses she has incurred. COB is used primarily for group policies, but it is also used for some individual policies.

To implement COB, claim examiners identify losses covered by two (or more) policies and apply rules that clearly divide the responsibility for payment between one insurer and another. Most group and some individual health insurance policies have COB provisions that establish these rules—that is, these provisions state what benefits the policy will pay if a loss is also covered by another policy. The provisions of different policies vary, but there is a considerable degree of uniformity, as most policies follow the guidelines of the National Association of Insurance Commissioners (NAIC).

COB rules work in this way: One policy is identified as the primary policy and the other as the secondary policy. The primary policy pays all the benefits it would normally pay if there were no additional coverage. The secondary policy pays additional benefits—exactly what benefits the secondary policy pays varies, but the total amount of benefits received by the insured never exceeds the actual amount of her expenses.

Which policy is primary and which is secondary is determined in the following way (according to NAIC guidelines): If only one of the two policies has a COB provision establishing procedures for coordinating benefits with other plans, the plan without such a provision is the primary policy and the other plan is the secondary policy. If both policies have COB provisions, the following rules are followed:

- **Dependent and nondependent coverage.** If the insured incurring the loss has dependent coverage under one policy (that is, he is the spouse or child of the employee or policyholder who has the coverage) and nondependent coverage under the other policy (that is, he is the employee or policyholder), the policy under which the person is not a dependent is the primary policy.
- **Dependent children.** If a child is covered as a dependent under both parents' health insurance coverage and the parents are not divorced or legally separated, the primary policy is that of the parent whose birthday falls earlier in the year.
- **Dependent children in the case of divorce or legal separation.** If a child is covered as a dependent under both parents' coverage and the parents are divorced or legally separated, the policy of the parent with custody is primary. If the child is also covered by the policy of the spouse of the parent with custody, the following order prevails: first, the policy of the parent with custody; second, the policy of the spouse of the parent with custody; and third, the policy of the parent without custody.

Coordination of benefits is an important part of claim processing. It is estimated that COB reduces claim payments by approximately 3 to 8 percent. These savings far outweigh the extra time spent implementing COB.

Once the benefit amount is determined, insured contributions (such as deductibles) accounted for, and the coordination of benefits paid by other policies completed, the amount of payment can be calculated and the claim paid.

Paying a Benefit or Denying a Claim

If the processing of a claim results in the determination that the claimed loss was covered by the policy, a benefit is paid. If processing reveals that the expense claimed is not covered by the policy, the claim is denied and no benefit is paid. Whether a benefit is paid or the claim denied, the insured is always informed in writing. He is sent a standard **explanation of benefits (EOB)** form or a letter.

To pay a benefit, two pieces of information are needed: the amount of payment (determined as described in the preceding section) and the party to whom payment should be made. This party is usually either the insured or the provider—which one is determined by the provisions of the policy as well as any assignments of benefits the insured may have made. If an assignment of benefits is made, benefits usually go to a provider, but they may be paid to another party, such as a creditor.

Notification of payment for tax purposes may also be necessary. Insurers are required to submit forms to the Internal Revenue Service for all providers to whom they pay more than $600 in benefit payments in a calendar year. The provider is also sent a copy of this notification.

Claim Investigations

The processing of a claim normally proceeds as described above. In some cases, however, an examiner may see indications that a claim is inaccurate or questionable in some substantial way. For example, he may suspect that services charged for were not actually provided, or that expenses are related to a preexisting condition that the insured did not declare in the application for insurance. In such cases, an investigation of the claim is initiated.

The extent of an investigation varies with the type of claim, the nature and amount of information required, and the difficulty in obtaining that information. An investigation can be limited to a letter or telephone call to a provider, or it might be more substantial, involving not only insurer personnel but also independent insurance adjusters and commercial inspection companies. Investigation of claims is covered in more detail in Chapter 12.

Hospital Audits

As a follow-up to claim processing, many insurance companies audit hospital bills to verify that the services and supplies that the insured has been charged for were actually provided and that the amounts charged are correct. Some companies automatically audit all bills over a certain amount (for example, $20,000). Others review bills over a certain amount to determine whether an audit is indicated.

Auditing may be done by insurer employees, or the insurer may hire an independent company specializing in this service. Some insurers encourage insureds to audit their own bills; if the insured finds an error, he is given a share of the money saved.

Claim Administration and Customer Service

Very often an insured has more contact with an insurer's claim department than with any other part of the company. As a result, the insured's overall opinion of the insurer may be to a very large extent a reflection of the service she receives from claim personnel. This means that claim administration is an area of opportunity for an insurer seeking to maintain and improve customer satisfaction. This can be done in various ways:

- Toll-free telephone lines to the claim department increase accessibility.
- Claim customer service units staffed by qualified personnel ensure that insureds' questions are answered correctly. Such a unit may be staffed by customer service representatives trained in claims or by claim examiners who take turns serving in the unit.
- Confusion and bad feeling on the part of insureds can often be avoided if explanations of benefits are clearly written and promptly sent.

Customer service typically focuses on individual insureds. But satisfaction on the part of group policyholder personnel, physicians and hospital staff, and insurance agents should also be a goal of any claim department.

Summary

The processing of a health insurance claim can be divided into three tasks:

- The claim examiner confirms the status of coverage—that is, she ascertains the date of the loss and the dates when coverage began and ended to determine whether coverage was in effect at the time of the loss. She must also note any indications that the policy may not be valid.
- The examiner determines if the specific loss claimed is covered by the policy. She examines the benefit provisions and other provisions of the policy and also confirms that all services provided were necessary.
- The examiner calculates the amount of benefit payment. To arrive at the correct amount, she takes into account the provisions of the policy and sometimes the normal charges for services. She also considers any contributions owed by the insured and any benefit payments made by other policies.

If a claim has suspicious characteristics, an investigation of it may be undertaken. Usually, however, a claim is processed normally and a benefit is paid or the claim is denied.

8 DISABILITY INCOME CLAIMS

- *Processing a Disability Claim*
- *Continuing Review of Disability Claims*
- *Tax Withholding from Benefits*

Introduction

Most kinds of health insurance help pay for the medical expenses an insured incurs when she falls ill, has an accident, or needs health care for some other reason. Disability income insurance, on the other hand, does not pay for medical expenses but rather replaces income lost by the insured when she is unable to work as a result of an accident or illness. Disability benefits are monthly payments of a preset amount, not the payment of actual expenses. Because of this basic difference, claim administration for disability income insurance differs in a number of ways from that of most other health coverages. For this reason, we examine disability claims in this separate chapter.

Processing a Disability Claim

Since most health coverages pay medical expenses, the processing of claims for these coverages involves (as we saw in the preceding chapter) determining what expenses have been incurred, whether they are covered by the policy, and what amount should be paid for them. The focus of disability claim processing, on the other hand, is not examining medical expenses but rather establishing whether the claimant (the insured) is in fact disabled—that is, whether she is unable to work due to an illness or injury.

Submitting a Claim

Submitting a disability claim includes, as for other kinds of claims, submitting notice of claim and proof of loss. For disability income insurance, proof of loss means proof that the claimant is disabled and unable to work, not proof that he has incurred any specific medical expense. Consequently, provider bills are not usually submitted.

The claimant submits proof of loss by completing the insurer's disability claim form. This form includes statements by the claimant, the attending physician (and any other health care providers), and sometimes the employer. The physician's statement describes the illness or injury, evaluates the claimant's condition and ability to work, and in some cases estimates the length of time the insured will not be able to work. The employer's statement indicates the date and reason the claimant stopped working.

Processing a Claim

As noted above, the focus in processing a disability claim is determining whether the claimant is disabled. However, before addressing this question, the claim examiner first verifies that if a disability does in fact exist, it is covered by the policy. This part of the process is similar to the examination of any other health insurance claim. The examiner checks the status of coverage to make sure the claimant was in fact covered by the policy at the time of loss. He also reviews the provisions of the policy to make sure coverage is not disallowed for some reason. For example, most policies exclude disabilities due to certain causes (such as a preexisting condition or a self-inflicted injury), and some individual policies cover only injuries or provide different benefits for injuries and illnesses.

After coverage is confirmed, the examiner determines whether the claimant is disabled. In making this determination, the examiner relies heavily on the attending physician's statement. However, it must be kept in mind that disability is not a purely medical question. Whether a person is unable to work depends not only on her medical condition but also on the duties of her occupation. In addition, whether a person is disabled under the terms of a policy depends on the definition of disability contained in that policy, and this definition varies. Thus, the physician's report is an important element in the determination of disability, but it is not the only consideration.

Furthermore, the examiner does not accept the judgment of the physician as readily as he might for another kind of claim. This is because, since the benefits for a disability claim are substantial monthly payments that may continue for a long period of time, an insurer can pay a very large total amount for a single disability claim. Therefore, disability claims are generally subject to greater scrutiny than other kinds of claims, and examiners often go to greater lengths to make sure such claims are valid.

Thus, if the attending physician's statement is inadequate or unclear in any way, the examiner must contact the physician for more information. The examiner must also request further information if the claim diverges from norms in any way—for example, if the amount of time the physician estimates that the disability will last is longer than normal for the claimant's condition.

Furthermore, if for any reason the examiner questions the attending physician's evaluation, the insurer may require the claimant to be examined by a physician it selects. This is known as an **independent medical examination**. Courts have held that independent medical examinations are reasonable and that insurers have the right to require them. If a claimant refuses to submit to such an examination, the processing of the claim and the payment of benefits can be delayed until he does so.

Prompt examination of disability claims is also very important. If a claim is not examined until the insured has recovered and returned to work, it may be difficult to determine if the claim was valid.

Continuing Review of Disability Claims

If an examiner approves a disability claim, the insurer begins making monthly (or in some cases weekly) benefit payments to the insured. These payments continue until the insured ceases to be disabled (or until the insured reaches the maximum amount of time or money allowed under the policy). Therefore, during the period when benefits are being paid, the examiner must periodically review the case to determine whether the insured is still disabled. In order to make this determination, the examiner usually requests reports from the attending physician, which he is allowed to do at reasonable intervals.

Residual Disability

In some cases, an insured is no longer totally disabled and can work, but because of a continuing condition he is not able to earn as much as before the disability, either because he cannot work as many hours or because he cannot perform the same duties as before. This situation is known as residual or permanent partial disability. Some policies pay benefits in such cases to make up for part of the insured's loss in earnings.

Residual disability presents a number of challenges to the claim examiner. Benefits are based on the amount of lost income, and that amount is calculated by subtracting the insured's current earnings from his predisability earnings. Therefore, the examiner must obtain accurate information on the insured's earnings both before the disability began and currently. He must also carefully monitor changes in the insured's current earnings, because if those earnings increase, the insured's disability-related loss of income is reduced, and his benefits, which are intended to compensate for that loss, must also be reduced. Finally, the claim examiner must monitor the insured's medical condition to confirm that his reduced earnings are in fact due to his medical condition.

Recurrent Disability

Disability income policies often have benefit periods—that is, for each claim there is a maximum period of time during which benefits will be paid. Therefore, when an insured goes through periods of disability separated by times when she is not disabled, the examiner must determine the following:

- Are all of the periods of disability part of one claim, so that they should be added together to determine if the benefit period has expired?
- Or is each period of disability part of a separate claim, so that a separate benefit period applies to each one?

For example, suppose a policy has a benefit period of two years. An insured suffered an injury, was disabled for 18 months, and then returned to work. After five months of work, he went on disability again and has been on disability for the last six months. If both periods of disability are considered part of the same claim, the insured has been on disability for two years for one claim, and his benefit period has expired. If the two periods are considered separate claims, the insured has been on disability for the second claim for only six months and so has 18 months left in his benefit period.

Determining whether two periods of disability are part of one claim or two can be difficult. The determination is based on the precise language of the policy and the facts of the individual case.

Tax Withholding from Benefits

Federal legislation requires insurers to withhold federal income tax from disability benefit payments if the insured requests it. Federal law also mandates that insurers withhold social security taxes from disability benefits in some cases. If withholding is done, the insurer is responsible for reporting and remitting taxes to the government.

Summary

Claim administration for disability income insurance differs in a number of ways from that of most other kinds of health insurance:

- In processing disability claims, the focus is on determining whether the claimant is disabled, not on examining expenses.
- Because of the very large amounts of benefits that are often at stake, disability claims are usually given closer scrutiny than other claims.
- Since disability benefit payments continue as long as the insured is disabled, the case must be periodically reviewed to confirm that the disability persists.
- To determine the amount of residual disability benefits, the examiner must take into account the insured's income.

9 CONTROLLING OPERATIONAL COSTS

- *Controlling Marketing, Sales, and Issuance Costs*
- *Controlling Underwriting Costs*
- *Controlling Claim Processing Costs*
- *Other Cost-Cutting Technology*

Introduction

The cost of health care has been increasing rapidly in recent decades. There are a number of reasons for this, such as overall inflation and the increased use of health care services. A key factor is the development of new therapies and diagnostic tools, including new technologies and drugs. These have made the treatment of many illnesses and injuries more effective but also much more expensive.

This rise in health care costs has led to a large increase in the claims made to health insurance companies and consequently in the premiums that insurers must charge in order to pay those claims. Higher premiums have meant that both individuals and businesses are spending a larger portion of their earnings on health insurance. More importantly, higher premiums have meant that many businesses can no longer afford to provide group insurance to their employees and many individuals can no longer afford to pay the premiums of either group or individual policies. As a result, while the number of people protected by health insurance has grown steadily in recent years, the number of people without coverage has also grown.

The health insurance industry is addressing this problem. Health insurance companies are working to control costs and keep premiums down. In doing so, they have taken two approaches: they have sought to make their own operations as efficient as possible, and they have structured their coverages to promote the cost-effective use of health care services. This chapter examines the first of these approaches, looking at a few of the ways insurers have held down the cost of doing business. The following chapter discusses the second approach.

Controlling Marketing, Sales, and Issuance Costs

The expenses of marketing, selling, and issuing new policies make up a major component of insurers' overall administrative costs. Of course, expenses of this sort are not incurred for continuing policies; therefore, the more continuing policies and the fewer new policies an insurer has, the lower overall expenses in this area will be. Consequently, the most effective way for an insurer to reduce these expenses is to increase the degree to which its policyholders continue their policies—that is, to improve persistency.

Sales personnel (the insurer's group representatives and agents) have the greatest impact on persistency. They can improve persistency by thoroughly understanding the insurer's products so that they sell each policyholder the product that best meets that policyholder's specific needs. In addition, they must maintain close contact with policyholders so that they can:

- reinforce the policyholder's recognition of the need to continue the coverage;
- be aware of any problems that arise and address them; and
- be aware of any changes in the needs of the policyholder and suggest modifications and additions in coverage to meet those needs.

To ensure that sales personnel perform in this way, thorough training is necessary.

Controlling Underwriting Costs

Underwriting is becoming more expensive due to higher salaries, rising overhead costs, and increases in the cost of medical examinations of applicants, attending physician statements, and inspection reports. Underwriting costs are particularly high for individual insurance, since each insured must be underwritten separately.

Underwriting costs can be reduced by:

- implementing an efficient and time-saving application processing system;
- introducing computerized systems that analyze underwriting data to determine if human intervention is needed; and
- focusing on training employees in the proper initial handling of applications, which can eliminate or substantially reduce delays and additional costs.

Controlling Claim Processing Costs

Insurers can reduce the cost of processing claims in a number of ways:

- They can organize claim processing units so that senior claim personnel, who have a great deal of training and experience and so are paid more, deal only with the small number of claims with complex problems. Associate claim examiners, with less training and experience and lower pay, should handle routine claims.
- They can concentrate claim operations in one large central office, which is less costly to operate than several field claim offices.
- They can introduce computerized systems. Such systems can perform electronic transmission of claims, automatic calculation of benefits, and automatic payment of claims.

The last of these approaches has had the greatest impact. Claim administration is an activity that is well suited to computerization, because it involves rule-based decision making and the processing of a high volume of transactions. Today, most insurers have fully computerized claim processing, implementing some or all of the following technologies:

- **Imaging** is a technology that converts paper documents into electronic documents that can be stored and retrieved electronically and viewed on a computer screen. Imaging allows a claim unit to shift from a labor-intensive paper filing system to an automated computer filing system.
- **Scanning**, like imaging, converts paper documents into electronic documents that can be stored and retrieved by computer, but scanning goes a step further— it converts data from these documents into electronic data that a computer can process. In this way, information from paper claim forms and other paper documents can be introduced into and used by the insurer's computerized claim processing system. This conversion formerly required many hours of data entry time.
- **Electronic claim processing** is the handling of a claim by computer, with little or no human involvement. The computer applies a set of rules to the data of a claim to determine whether benefits should be paid and what the amount should be. The computer also produces benefit checks, explanations of benefits, and necessary letters, and stores information about the claim.
- **Fraud detection software** works like electronic claim processing in that a computer applies a set of rules to the data of a claim. But in fraud detection software, these rules identify claims with characteristics that are often associated with fraud. These cases can then be investigated.

- An **expert disability system** is a computer program that applies a set of rules to the data of a claim (such as diagnosis, age, and occupation) to estimate the duration of disability.
- An **automated repetitive payment system** automatically pays benefits on a regular basis for a predetermined period of time. It is most often used to make monthly disability payments until the time at which the case needs to be reviewed.

Other Cost-Cutting Technology

We have seen how new technologies have been used to cut costs in the underwriting and claim areas. Technology has had a major impact on costs in other operational areas as well. For example, the scanning systems used for claim forms can be used for enrollment forms. **Automated voice response systems (AVRS)** can reduce personnel costs in areas that involve customer service. And electronic mail (e-mail) and insurer Internet sites make communication not only quicker and more effective but also much cheaper. Looking toward the future, it is clear that those insurers who stay on the cutting edge of technological innovations will have an advantage in offering quality service at a competitive price.

Summary

Insurance companies are striving to control the cost of health insurance. One of the ways insurers do this is by cutting their own administrative and claim processing costs. There are a number of ways to do this, including training sales personnel to improve persistency and reorganizing underwriting and claim units for greater efficiency. But the approach that has had the greatest impact in all administrative and claim areas is the introduction of new technology.

10 PROMOTING COST-EFFECTIVE HEALTH CARE

- *Cost Sharing*
- *Targeted Incentives for Cost-Effective Alternatives*
- *Case Management*
- *Wellness Programs*

Introduction

In the preceding chapter we looked at ways insurers hold down the cost of health insurance by controlling their own operational costs. Such efforts can have a significant impact, but they do not address the main cause of increasing health insurance costs—the rising cost of health care.

How can we deal with this problem? No one would propose that we cut costs by not providing people with the best medical care available. Better health and longer life are among the great achievements of our modern civilization, and we all look forward to even more progress. What then can we do?

We can limit the cost of health care to what is really necessary for improved health. We can do this by seeking to ensure that the best health care available is provided in the most efficient and least wasteful way possible. In other words, we can promote the practice of high-quality, cost-effective health care.

In practice, providing high-quality, cost-effective health care means two things: using the most effective means of diagnosis and treatment while at the same time avoiding unnecessary medical services; and, in cases in which two alternative treatments are possible, *both equally effective from a medical point of view but not equally economical*, taking the more economical approach.

How can insurers promote cost-effective health care? One important way is encouraging consumers and health care providers to make smart choices. Two examples:

- People sometimes seek treatment in a hospital emergency room when they could be cared for in a physician's office just as quickly and effectively and much less expensively. Insurers can give insureds financial incentives to avoid this unnecessary use of expensive services.

- Physicians sometimes request surgery in cases where drug therapy is not only less costly but has been determined by medical experts to be more effective. Insurers can inform physicians about such alternatives and encourage them to use them when appropriate.

There are other ways to promote cost-effective health care as well. In this chapter, we examine the incentives insurers can give insureds to make cost-effective choices, and we look at two other approaches, case management and wellness programs.

Cost Sharing

One way of encouraging insureds to make cost-effective choices is having them share the cost of health care. If insureds pay a portion of costs, they have a financial incentive to keep those costs down and so are more likely to avoid using unnecessary services. This approach is known as cost sharing and includes the use of deductibles, coinsurance, and copayments. We have discussed these arrangements before but will review them briefly here.

- A **deductible** is an amount of covered expenses that an insured must pay before the insurer pays benefits. For example, if a policy has a $500 deductible, the insured must pay the first $500 of covered expenses he incurs, at which point he is said to have satisfied the deductible and the insurer begins paying covered expenses.
- **Coinsurance** is a form of cost sharing in which, after the deductible is satisfied, the insurer and the insured each pays a percentage of covered expenses. The insured's share is much less than the insurer's—typically, the insured pays 20 or 25 percent.
- A **copayment** is a flat dollar amount that an insured pays for a type of service. It is not a percentage of costs, like coinsurance, but is always the same amount no matter what the actual cost of the service. For example, a policy might require insureds to pay $10 for each visit to physician's office. The insured would always pay $10, whatever the actual cost to the insurer of the office visit.

Cost sharing has been practiced for many years. However, in response to the recent increases in health care costs, insurers have increased cost sharing in order to increase the incentives that insureds have to use health care services prudently.

Targeted Incentives for Cost-Effective Alternatives

Cost sharing is a broad approach to encouraging cost-effective choices. It gives insureds incentives to hold down their health care expenditures in a general way, but it does not encourage or discourage the use of any particular service or treatment. There is also a more targeted approach. Insurers can identify specific health care services that are cost-effective and others that are not and give insureds incentives to choose the cost-effective alternatives.

A number of examples of this approach can be found in the area of hospital care. In this section we look at some of the cost-effective alternatives to hospital care and how insurers encourage their use.

Outpatient Care and Outpatient Surgery

Much of the diagnosis, treatment, and rehabilitation that has historically taken place in hospitals can be provided on an outpatient basis. Outpatient surgery is also becoming safe and appropriate in an increasing number of cases, as new surgical techniques and anesthetics allow quick recovery. The savings gained by eliminating the high costs of hospital room and board are considerable, and insurers are structuring policies to give insureds incentives to use outpatient care. For example, insurers often reduce deductibles and coinsurance if surgery is performed on an outpatient basis.

Birthing Centers

Birthing centers are a less expensive alternative to hospitalization for low-risk deliveries and postpartum newborn care. They are usually located near and have a relationship with a full-service hospital, so that a quick transfer can be made if complications occur. Many insurers encourage the use of birthing centers by waiving deductibles and/or coinsurance.

Alcohol and Drug Treatment Facilities

Patients with drug and alcohol problems can often be treated more effectively and less expensively in a specialized facility rather than in a hospital. In addition to providing the detoxification services of a hospital, these facilities offer counseling to help patients confront and deal with their dependency, making long-term recovery more likely. Many insurers have recognized this and encourage the use of approved facilities.

Hospices

Hospice care is an alternative to hospital care for terminally ill patients. Hospice care is less costly and offers a number of advantages for dying patients, such as a focus on relieving the patient's pain and discomfort and addressing the emotional and spiritual needs of both the patient and his family. Many insurers have restructured their policies to encourage the use of hospice care.

Centers of Excellence

Centers of excellence are an alternative to hospital care for patients with difficult-to-treat or rare medical conditions. They are medical institutions that provide advanced forms of treatment, such as organ transplants and cancer therapies. The quality of care in these centers is high. In addition, because centers of excellence specialize in certain advanced treatments, they are often able to provide these treatments more economically than hospitals that perform them less frequently.

Skilled Nursing Facilities and Home Health Care

Sometimes a person does not need the level of care provided by a hospital but is not well enough to survive at home with no professional care at all. In the past, such people often remained in a hospital unnecessarily because there was no appropriate place for them to go or because their insurance paid only for hospitalization. Alternatives are now more common, and health insurance policies usually reimburse for them and often encourage their use.

One alternative is a skilled nursing facility. Such facilities provide all the care many patients need, but per-day charges are lower than hospital room and board charges. For other patients who need even less care, home health care may be more appropriate. In home health care, visiting nurses or home health aides working under the supervision of a registered nurse provide part-time or intermittent care to the patient in her own home. Home health care is less expensive than either hospital care or a skilled nursing facility. Advances in home therapy, such as home dialysis, have made home health care an option for an increasing number of people.

Case Management

Case management is a method of improving both the quality and the cost-effectiveness of health care. However, case management promotes cost-effectiveness in a different way from the approaches we have discussed so far in this chapter. It does not work primarily by encouraging insureds to make cost-effective choices, but rather it identifies and eliminates redundant and overlapping health care services.

A person with a catastrophic or long-term medical condition is typically cared for by many different health care providers, and it is difficult for a single provider (such as the patient's personal physician) to keep track of all the many medical services the patient receives. This lack of coordination can lead to the overlapping of services given by different providers or to gaps in services. The result is health care that is neither the most medically effective nor the most cost-effective.

Case management addresses this problem. In case management, one individual, usually a nurse coordinator, is given the responsibility of monitoring and coordinating all the services provided to the patient in order to ensure that she receives all the services she needs, that she is cared for in the most appropriate setting, and that she does not receive redundant services. In this way, case management promotes both quality and cost-effectiveness.

Of course, for the great majority of insureds, case management is not necessary—assigning a professional to coordinate a person's medical care makes sense only when many services are being provided by many providers, and this occurs only in the relatively uncommon instance of a catastrophic or long-term medical condition. But such conditions, though infrequent, require many resources over a long period of time and so can account for a large proportion of health care costs. Consequently, case management has great potential for cost savings.

To make the most of this potential, insurance companies seek to identify cases appropriate to case management and offer case management services to the insured. Some insurers automatically flag all cases with certain characteristics and consider them for case management. For example, a case might be flagged whenever any single claim is above a certain amount (such as $50,000), or when the claims for any individual total more that a certain amount (such as $100,000), or when a claim is made for one of a list of specified medical conditions. Alternatively, the insured himself or his family or physician may request case management services. Identification of cases should be done early, if possible even before the first hospital admission, to maximize quality of care and cost savings.

Despite the potential for cost control, most insurers do not obligate insureds to accept case management services. However, insureds generally like case management because of the improvement in quality resulting from the elimination of overlapping and gaps in services. In addition, case management offers insureds a number of other advantages:

- Insureds often find dealing with many different providers confusing and frustrating. Case management offers assistance with this.
- Without case management, an insured may make decisions and handle his situation in a haphazard way, often simply reacting to a series of events and

recommendations without having a clear overall understanding of his case and the options open to him. Case management is designed to give the insured a full understanding of his circumstances, to keep him informed of his progress and his choices at each stage, and to assist him and his family in making decisions.

- Some case management programs provide coverage for services that the regular health insurance plan does not (for example, alternatives to hospitalization such as home health care).

Wellness Programs

The methods of controlling health care costs discussed in the preceding sections of this chapter all have one thing in common—they focus on ensuring that once a person falls ill, health care services are provided in a cost-effective way. Another way to cut health care costs is to help people avoid becoming ill in the first place.

Of course, many medical conditions are unavoidable, but others are connected to behaviors such as smoking, drinking to excess, overeating, eating an unhealthy diet, and failing to exercise. Changes in a person's behavior can make such conditions much less likely to occur. Other conditions are not related to behavior, but if they are detected early, relatively minor treatment can keep them from becoming a serious problem. For these conditions, regular examinations and testing can make a difference.

To encourage and help insureds to improve their own health and prevent illness, many insurers have instituted wellness programs. These programs typically provide information on how behavior and lifestyle affect health and how to make changes. They sometimes offer physical examinations and disease screening at no charge. Some wellness programs are jointly sponsored by insurers and employers, and these may even offer some financial assistance to insureds who participate in programs for losing weight, quitting smoking, or improving fitness.

Wellness programs can not only cut health care costs, but also, and more importantly, they improve the health and the quality of life for insureds who participate in them.

Summary

The rise in health insurance costs of recent decades is largely the result of the rising cost of health care. Consequently, although insurers can help keep health insurance premiums affordable by controlling their operational costs, the most effective way to hold premium rates down is to promote the practice of high-quality, cost-effective health care. Practicing cost-effective care means using the most effective means of treatment and diagnosis while avoiding unnecessary services and, in cases in which two alternatives are possible and both are equally effective from a medical point of view but not equally economical, taking the more economical approach.

Insurers can promote cost-effective health care by giving consumers incentives to make cost-effective choices. Requiring insureds to share the cost of health care by paying deductibles, coinsurance, and copayments is a broad approach that encourages insureds to keep expenditures down without focusing on specific alternatives. Insurers also create targeted incentives by structuring the benefit provisions of policies to give insureds a financial advantage if they use cost-effective alternatives (such as outpatient care, outpatient surgery, birthing centers, drug and alcohol treatment facilities, hospices, centers of excellence, skilled nursing facilities, and home health care). Insurers can also promote cost-effective care by establishing case management and wellness programs. In case management, health care services are managed both to enhance the quality of care and to avoid overlapping and unnecessary services. Wellness programs encourage healthy behavior and early detection in order to prevent illness before it occurs.

11 HEALTH INSURANCE FRAUD AND ABUSE

- *Defining Fraud and Abuse*
- *Provider Fraud and Abuse*
- *Consumer Fraud and Abuse*
- *Motor Vehicle Accidents*

Introduction

In the last two chapters, we looked at a number of ways insurers work to hold down health insurance costs and premiums. In this chapter and the next, we discuss another way to reduce costs—by fighting health insurance fraud and abuse. The potential for savings in this area is substantial, as fraud and abuse contribute significantly to the cost of health insurance—for example, the General Accounting Office estimated in a 1992 report to Congress that they account for 10 percent of the nation's health care spending.

This chapter examines how health insurance fraud and abuse occur. The following chapter looks at insurers' efforts to detect and prevent fraud and abuse.

Defining Fraud and Abuse

There are many definitions of health insurance fraud, including legal definitions embodied in various laws and regulations. However, all of these definitions have the same basic elements: a person knowingly and intentionally deceives another in order to gain a health insurance benefit that he is not legitimately entitled to.

Sometimes, people use the health insurance system in illegitimate ways, but their actions do not meet any legal definition of fraud. Typically, they seek to obtain benefits that they are not entitled to, but they do not knowingly and intentionally deceive or make any misrepresentations. Such actions are usually referred to as health insurance abuse.

Two examples will clarify the distinction between fraud and abuse:

- A surgeon deliberately submits a bill for a procedure that he did not perform. This is *fraud* because the surgeon is knowingly and intentionally making a misrepresentation.
- A surgeon performs a procedure and deliberately submits a bill for much more than he usually charges. This is *not fraud*, because the surgeon is making no misrepresentation—he is simply billing a certain amount for a service that he did in fact provide. This is *abuse*, however, because the surgeon is intentionally trying to obtain more than he is entitled to.

The distinction between fraud and abuse is important, because fraud is subject to criminal prosecution, while abuse is not. If abuse occurs, the insurer may seek to recover benefits that should not have been paid, but a crime has not been committed. In the case of fraud, a crime has occurred and law enforcement agencies may be notified.

In this chapter, we discuss a number of methods used to obtain health insurance benefits illegitimately. Most of these methods could involve either fraud or abuse, and whether it is fraud or abuse that has occurred in a particular case depends on the facts of the case.

The National Health Care Anti-Fraud Association (NHCAA) defines health care fraud as follows:

Health care fraud is an intentional deception or misrepresentation that an individual or entity makes, knowing that the misrepresentation could result in some unauthorized benefit to the individual, or the entity, or to some other party.

Provider Fraud and Abuse

Although the vast majority of physicians and organizations providing health care are honest, a few providers do commit fraud and abuse in various ways.

Billing Schemes

Some health care providers submit bills to insurers for amounts that they are not entitled to. The provider may charge for a service she did not in fact provide or charge too much for a service that was provided. Such acts are known as billing schemes.

Billing schemes often involve **billing codes**. Billing codes are numerical codes (or sometimes number-and-letter codes), each of which corresponds to a medical or surgical service or procedure. They are used to submit bills in the standardized formats used by insurers and were devised to make claim processing more efficient and cut costs.

The Physicians' Current Procedural Terminology, published by the American Medical Association, includes detailed descriptions of the services and procedures that correspond to each code so that providers can submit the proper code for the service they have provided. However, both honest mistakes and fraudulent claims occur, and because coded bills are processed by standardized procedures or even automated systems, they may not be detected.

There are several types of billing schemes:

- **Billing for services not provided.** For example, a laboratory might submit a bill for a large number of tests, some of which were performed and others not. Or a bill might be submitted for a full operating room setup when only less expensive equipment was used.
- **Upcoding.** Upcoding occurs when a provider submits a bill for a service that is similar to but more expensive than the service she actually provided. (It is called upcoding because the bill uses the code for a higher-priced service instead of the correct code.) For example, a physician may charge for a comprehensive physical exam when only a limited physical was performed. Or she may charge for an extensive office visit when only a routine visit occurred.
- **Unbundling of charges.** Some major surgical operations are made up of several lesser procedures. For example, a total hysterectomy includes removal of the ovaries, removal of the fallopian tubes, removal of the appendix, and removal of the uterus. If all of the procedures are performed at the same time as part of one operation, the provider must submit one charge for the whole operation. If procedures are performed separately, the provider may submit separate charges. Since it costs more to perform the procedures separately than all at the same time, a provider will be paid more for separate procedures. Therefore, to obtain a larger payment, some providers falsely submit a bill with separate charges for each procedure even though all were performed together. This is known as unbundling of charges.
- **Billing for noncovered treatments.** Sometimes providers bill for treatments that are not covered by the insured's policy. They do this by using codes for similar treatments that are covered. This approach is typically used to bill for **unproven treatments** (also called **alternative** or **experimental treatments**). These are procedures and medicines that have not been tested and established by the proper professional or regulatory authorities as effective and safe. Such

treatments are not covered by health insurance policies, so the only way a provider can charge for them is to disguise them in his bill as another treatment.

Overutilization of Services

In some cases, medical providers commit abuse not by incorrect billing but by overutilization of services. That is, they provide all the services they bill for and they bill correctly, but in order to earn more money, they provide services that are not needed. Some examples:

• A patient is given diagnostic tests that have no relevance to his condition.
• A patient is kept in a hospital or other facility longer than necessary.
• Physical therapy or chiropractic care is provided longer than the patient needs it.

Overutilization can involve fraud, but more commonly it is a form of abuse, since the provider does not usually misrepresent the services she has provided or the patient's condition.

Medical experts have created standard guidelines stating which treatments and tests are normally appropriate for which medical conditions and how long hospital care and therapy are normally needed in given cases. If a provider's services fall outside these guidelines, she is not necessarily overutilizing. There may be complications or unusual circumstances that justify special treatment, additional testing, or longer hospitalization. And even when a provider is overutilizing, she is not necessarily engaging in abuse. Although she is providing unneeded services, she may be doing so not for financial gain but because it is her honest medical judgment that the services are necessary. In other cases providers overutilize because they fear that their patients will claim that not enough was done to diagnose or treat a condition and charge them with malpractice. (Overutilization done for this reason is known as **defensive medicine**.)

However, there are other instances in which providers clearly perform unneeded services with the intent of making illegitimate financial gains. An example would be a physician who requires all new patients to undergo $2,000 worth of lab tests, X-rays, and physical exams without regard to diagnosis or symptoms. Another example is a provider who repeatedly provides services not in keeping with guidelines and is able to offer no medical justification for these services when questioned.

Waiving Out-of-Pocket Payments

As we have seen, most insurance policies encourage cost-effective health care by requiring insureds to pay a part of their medical expenses in the form of deductibles, copayments, or coinsurance. Some physicians, dentists, podiatrists, chiropractors, hospitals, diagnostic centers, and other providers advertise that they do not require patients to make these out-of-pocket payments. Some providers also guarantee that a patient will have to pay nothing herself, even if expenses exceed the benefits of her policy, by agreeing to accept whatever her policy pays as full payment.

In some cases, this practice in itself constitutes health insurance fraud, as it violates regulations or contracts. In other cases, it is legal, but even then it is often associated with fraud and abuse. This is because many of the providers who waive out-of-pocket payments by patients use fraudulent activities to offset the cost. Insurers must be aware of this practice and must subject those who engage in it to close scrutiny.

Consumer Fraud and Abuse

False or Altered Bills

As we saw in Chapter Seven, health insurance benefits are now most often paid to providers rather than insureds. However, there are still cases where insureds pay providers for services, submit proof of that payment (usually in the form of a provider's bill) to the insurer, and are reimbursed by the insurer. In such cases, insureds can submit false bills for services they never received and never paid for, then pocket the money paid by the insurer. In other cases, the insured does in fact pay for medical services, but he alters the provider's bills to show that he received more expensive services than those actually provided. The insured is reimbursed for the higher-priced service, reimburses the provider for the cheaper service, and keeps the difference.

False and altered bills are particularly common among the claims filed by persons in foreign countries against U.S. insurers. Claims from certain countries in particular are very commonly fraudulent. In fact, some countries have become notorious— fake forms, seals, and rubber-stamp signatures are readily available there, and even kits and classes for those wishing to file bogus claims.

Insurance Speculation

In Chapter Seven we also discussed overinsurance, the phenomenon whereby the same expense is covered by two or more insurance policies. As we saw, this typically occurs when a husband and wife both have dependent coverage from their group plan, or when an individual is covered by both a group plan and an individual policy or by two group plans. Coordination of benefit arrangements are usually effective in ensuring that double benefits are not paid.

However, some people deliberately buy many policies covering the same expenses and do not report each policy to the insurers providing the other policies as they are required to do. They then submit claims for the same loss under all these policies with the intention of making a substantial amount of money. This sort of scheme is known as insurance speculation.

Fraudulent Disability Claims

Disability income insurance fraud can take several forms. The insured may maintain that he is not well enough to work when he in fact is. In cases where the level of benefits depends on the insured's income, he may lie about this. Or the insured may claim that a disability is due to a cause covered by the policy when it is actually the result of an excluded cause (such as a preexisting condition).

Disability fraud presents several problems to insurers:

- It can be difficult to prove that someone is able to work. This determination is not always clear-cut, and honest and reasonable physicians may disagree on the extent of an individual's impairment.
- The difficulty of determining disability is increased by the lack of a clear definition of disability in many policies. If a policy has a vague definition, it is harder to prove that an insured does not fit that definition. Insurers are realizing that a policy must define disability very specifically in terms of what duties an insured can and cannot perform and what alternative occupations are acceptable.
- The temptation of fraud is greater for disability insurance. Fraudulent claims for most other kinds of health insurance usually produce limited amounts of money, but disability fraud offers the prospect of not having to work for a long period of time.

Motor Vehicle Accidents

Some fraudulent claims are related to phony motor vehicle accidents. Consumers and providers work together along with others in such schemes, which are of two main types:

- **Actual accidents.** Participants deliberately cause accidents, sometimes involving themselves only, at other times involving an unsuspecting third driver who is caused to rear-end one of the participants' cars. In either case, the car that is hit has several occupants, all of whom may claim injuries.
- **Paper accidents.** Two or more car owners conspire to report an accident that did not occur, and one driver claims fault. Already damaged cars are used, or cars are damaged intentionally.

In both cases, a provider involved in the scheme provides documentation of injuries that did not occur and submits bills for services that were never provided.

Dishonest attorneys pursue these cases with full knowledge that they are fraudulent. Once benefits have been paid, they are divided among those involved. Such a conspiracy is known as **collusion**—a secret collaboration of two or more parties for fraudulent purposes.

Summary

A major component of the cost of health care and health insurance is fraud and abuse. Fraud occurs when a person knowingly and intentionally deceives another in order to gain a health insurance benefit that he is not legitimately entitled to. Abuse occurs when a person seeks to obtain a benefit that he is not entitled to, but he does not intentionally deceive. Fraud and abuse may be committed by providers, consumers, or others. Provider fraud and abuse includes billing schemes such as upcoding, unbundling, billing for services not provided, and billing for noncovered treatments. Overutilization of services can also be a form of provider abuse. Consumer fraud and abuse include submitting false or altered bills, engaging in insurance speculation, and falsely claiming to be disabled. Both providers and consumers can be involved in motor vehicle accident schemes.

12 PREVENTING FRAUD AND ABUSE

- *Insurer Anti-Fraud Measures*
- *Fraud Detection and Investigation*
- *Government Involvement in Fraud Prevention*
- *Insurance Industry Associations*

Introduction

Insurance companies recognize the substantial cost of health insurance fraud and abuse and the impact they have on the affordability of health insurance. Consequently, insurers have always devoted considerable resources to the prevention of fraud and abuse. Moreover, in recent years insurers have intensified their anti-fraud efforts and adopted new methods, approaches, and technologies.

In this chapter, we examine the anti-fraud measures taken by insurers. We also look at how the types of fraud and abuse described in the preceding chapter are typically detected and investigated. (For the sake of brevity, we sometimes refer to fraud only, but it should be assumed that both fraud and abuse are meant.)

Insurer Anti-Fraud Measures

Insurers combat fraud and abuse in a number of ways:

- **Training employees.** Insurers train their claim personnel and others in how fraudulent schemes and practices work. These employees are sometimes able to detect fraud themselves; in other cases, they can identify cases where fraud may be occurring and pass them to an investigator.
- **Screening claims.** Insurers commonly screen claims as they are received for indications of possible errors or fraud. If such indications exist, the claim can be looked at more closely or even investigated. Computer programs are often used for screening.

- **Auditing claims.** Insurers also regularly subject representative samples of their claims to in-depth audits. This enables them to identify errors and sometimes fraud.
- **Creating special investigative units (SIUs).** SIUs are groups within an insurance company that are made up of personnel trained and experienced in fraud and have the primary responsibility of investigating suspicious claims. The formation of SIUs has intensified in recent years, so that now almost all insurers have them, and this has been a major factor in the increased prevention of fraud.
- **Using outside services.** It is not always economically feasible for insurers to develop specialized personnel or units that can handle all types of fraud investigation work. For this reason, they often work with outside firms such as surveillance specialists and foreign investigators.
- **Using information databases.** Much of the information needed to investigate claims can be found in databases maintained by government agencies, independent bureaus, and commercial services. Advances in technology have made such databases even more useful in recent years, as they now contain more information and are easier to use.
- **Cooperating with other insurers.** Insurers share information with other insurers and sometimes collaborate on cases with them. Many insurance companies work together within the framework of industry associations and task forces.
- **Enlisting consumer cooperation.** Insurers try to educate insureds about the cost of fraud and ask them to report cases of fraud that come to their attention. Some insurers maintain hotlines for the reporting of such information. Insurers also sometimes ask insureds to audit their own bills and pay the insured a share of any savings that may result.
- **Reporting to and working with government agencies.** Insurers report cases of criminal fraud to the appropriate law enforcement organizations and state insurance bureaus and share information with them. Government agencies, like insurers, have intensified their anti-fraud efforts in recent years.

Fraud Detection and Investigation

A case of fraud or abuse is most typically detected in this way: If a claim has a certain characteristic, it is more likely to be fraudulent than a claim without that characteristic. For example, if a claim includes a bill for a service not normally associated with the diagnosis listed on the claim, the claim may be legitimate (there may be special circumstances that made the service necessary), but it is more likely than the average claim to be fraudulent, and it should be investigated. Such characteristics are known as **red flags**. Claim personnel are taught what these red flags are, and they identify claims that have them. Computerized claim screening programs can also identify claims with red flags.

When claims with suspicious characteristics are identified, they are passed to an investigator and an investigation is initiated. That is, the investigator seeks more information about the case to determine if, in fact, fraud or abuse has occurred. An investigation can be very limited, consisting simply of writing a letter to or telephoning a hospital or a physician to request information. Or it can be more extensive, involving the collection of large amounts of information and the participation of outside investigators or law enforcement agencies.

An investigation always results in an investigative report. This report both determines the insurer's action on the case and becomes the basis for the insurer's legal case should a lawsuit or criminal prosecution become necessary.

Identifying questionable claims can add considerable time to the claim process. Insurers must balance the gains realized against the hours spent by claim personnel. However, software screening programs have been developed that can perform much of this work quickly and cheaply. These programs are becoming more sophisticated and are increasingly able to accommodate substantial amounts of data, conduct extensive database searches, and address complex, subtle, and costly fraud schemes.

In this section, we examine in more detail the detection of the types of fraud and abuse we discussed in the last chapter.

False or Altered Bills

For some false or altered bills, the red flags are obvious—a document may have typewriter strike-overs, correction fluid changes, different colored inks, or non-matching fonts. Or the signature of the insured or the provider may be missing. Or photocopies may be submitted instead of originals. Claim personnel turn such claims over to an investigator.

Other false or altered bills are not physically obvious because they have been skillfully prepared by professional criminals. However, in such cases specialized equipment can reveal forgeries. For example, a video spectral comparator uses various wavelengths of light to see through papers and inks to determine if alterations were made.

But the examination of physical documents, whether done by the naked eye or technologically, is becoming less and less relevant as the health insurance industry moves from submitting claims on paper to submitting claims electronically. Fortunately, however, there are red flags related to the facts of the case rather than the physical characteristics of documents. Some of these include:

- Bills are shown as already paid in cash.
- In a case where benefits would normally be assigned to a provider, they are unassigned and so must be paid directly to the insured.

- The services claimed are inconsistent with the diagnosis.
- Physicians' bills show many visits, but no bills for prescription or other related expenses are submitted.

As with other kinds of fraud, if one of these red flags is detected, the claim is passed to an investigator, who seeks more information. It should be kept in mind that a claim with one or more of these characteristics is not necessarily fraudulent, only more likely to be so than the average claim.

Billing Fraud

Fraud is detected in bills from providers in much the same way as in claims submitted by insureds—typically, bills are identified by claim personnel or a screening program as having a suspicious characteristic (such as a service not matching a diagnosis, or separate billing of a number of services that might be part of one major procedure). The bill is passed to an investigator, who may contact the provider for more information. The investigator may also review the medical records of the insured. These records show the condition of the patient and the health care services she received, and this information should match the facts stated in the bill.

Insurance Speculation

Cases of insurance speculation usually come to light when a claim examiner notices on a provider's bill an indication of a second insurer that the insured did not declare. He passes the bill to a fraud investigator, who contacts the other insurance company for verification that overinsurance in fact exists. If there is a suspicion of fraud, other insurers will usually share records and exchange information.

Motor Vehicle Accident Fraud

The common characteristics of fraudulent claims involving motor vehicle accidents include the following:

- Subjective injuries such as neck or back sprain are claimed.
- Soft-tissue injuries are claimed. (They do not show up on X-rays.)
- The same medical provider is used for many auto accident claims.
- The police report is filed at a police station rather than at the scene of the accident.

Foreign Claim Fraud

Fraudulent foreign claims also have certain common characteristics. For example, frequent diagnoses include hepatitis and injuries resulting from a motor vehicle accident. Claims for lengthy hospital stays in Africa or the Middle East, where it is often difficult to get medical records, are also common.

Insurers often do not have the internal resources to investigate a foreign claim and so hire a firm specializing in this area. Many of these firms are based in the United States but work with investigators in foreign countries. Foreign investigations may take weeks or months to complete, especially if the work involves medical facilities in remote locations.

Disability Fraud

Because disability claims can involve very large amounts of money, insurers are particularly concerned with identifying fraud in this area. Some common steps that are taken if a claim is suspicious:

- The insurer requires the insured to submit to an independent medical examination.
- The insurer requests and reviews medical records and reports from physicians on an on-going basis.
- A case manager is hired to fully assess the authenticity of the disability and the abilities and needs of the insured.
- Surveillance of the insured is conducted to determine whether his behavior indicates that he is able to work. For example, an insured who claims he cannot work because he cannot engage in strenuous physical activities may be photographed or videotaped participating in such activities. Surveillance may be done by insurer personnel or by a contracted outside investigator.

These methods are often expensive and may add considerably to the overall cost of doing business in this field.

Records and Databases

Investigators often find valuable information in public records and commercial databases. Public records include court records, marriage and death records, and motor vehicle records (which may be useful in accident cases). Databases include the National Insurance Crime Bureau (NICB), the Property Insurance Loss Register (PILR), and the Central Index Bureau (CIB). These databases contain information on insurance policy numbers and claim histories and may note past convictions or suspicion of fraudulent activity. Databases are growing in importance—new technology has made them easier to use and increased the amount of information they can contain, and the Internet has made them much more accessible.

Government Involvement in Fraud Prevention

Federal, state, and local governments and law enforcement agencies work closely with insurance companies to deter fraud. The different levels of government have also enacted laws that can be used to force restitution of funds and to impose monetary fines, prison sentences, and the revocation of professional licenses. A few of the most important agencies and laws are discussed below.

Government Agencies

Several agencies of the federal government deal with the types of health insurance fraud that relate to their area of activity. For example, the Department of Health and Human Services works to prevent Medicare or Medicaid fraud. However, the Federal Bureau of Investigation serves as the umbrella organization in this field— it works with all agencies and has the authority to investigate all types of health insurance fraud.

A growing number of states have **state fraud bureaus** (or agencies). These bureaus engage in a variety of activities:

- They collect information from insurance companies on suspicious claims. (Insurers are granted immunity against lawsuits for libel or slander for any information they submit.)
- They investigate cases, sometimes in collaboration with local and federal authorities.
- They promote anti-fraud training for law enforcement personnel, insurer personnel, members of the media, and judges and prosecutors.

State fraud bureaus often impose requirements on insurers that involve the reporting of information, the staffing levels of SIUs, and the training of SIU staff and other insurer personnel. Since each state bureau has different requirements, this has created a burden for insurers.

Legislation

The National Association of Insurance Commissioners (NAIC) has drafted model laws relating to insurance fraud. The federal government and state governments are influenced by these models when they enact their own laws in this area.

The Health Insurance Portability and Accountability Act of 1996 (HIPAA) includes an extensive set of anti-fraud provisions:

- It establishes a program to coordinate the efforts of federal, state, and local law enforcement programs working to control health insurance fraud.

- It establishes a national health insurance fraud and abuse data collection program. All government agencies and insurers are required to report to this program any adverse action taken against a health care provider, supplier, or practitioner.
- It adds to the U.S. Code the federal offense of health care fraud. This offense pertains to fraud in any health care benefit program, public or private.

Insurance Industry Associations

Insurance companies work together to combat fraud and abuse. They share information and sometimes investigate and prosecute cases together. They also join forces in insurance industry associations.

The Health Insurance Association of America (HIAA)

The Health Insurance Association of America (HIAA) is the nation's most prominent trade association representing private health insurers. HIAA is engaged in a number of efforts in the area of health insurance fraud and abuse, which are developed, implemented, and overseen by the organization's Joint Subcommittee on Fraud and Abuse. This committee's goals are to:

- increase public awareness of fraud and abuse through educational programs;
- use lobbying resources to strengthen laws pertaining to health care fraud; and
- encourage stronger fraud and abuse detection and prevention activities by state medical and professional boards.

HIAA also participates in various federal task forces studying health care abuse and fraud and testifies at congressional hearings about issues and legislation affecting health care fraud efforts.

The National Health Care Anti-Fraud Association (NHCAA)

The National Health Care Anti-Fraud Association (NHCAA) was founded in 1985 by several private health insurers and federal and state law enforcement officials. It is an issue-based organization made up of private and public sector individuals and organizations and focusing on the detection, investigation, and prosecution of health care fraud.

NHCAA conducts national seminars on the most effective methods of combating health care fraud. Special emphasis is placed on education and detection, investigation, prosecution, and prevention of fraud. Training workshops are featured at NHCAA's annual meeting.

An information-sharing network is available to NHCAA members to aid in the investigation of fraud cases. Assistance to law enforcement agencies in their investigation and prosecution of health care fraud also is provided.

The International Claim Association (ICA)

The International Claim Association's Fraud and Claim Abuse Committee was established to educate, inform, and encourage insurers to step up anti-fraud efforts. The ICA holds an annual conference where fraud issues are discussed and debated. Publications distributed by the ICA feature original articles on fraud and abuse written by employees of member companies of the organization.

Regional Associations

In recent years, several regional associations and task forces have been formed. These organizations are made up of insurers, government entities, and law enforcement agencies and facilitate the sharing of information and the collaboration on cases among these parties. Such organizations include the Midwest Anti-Fraud Association, the Anti-Fraud Association of the Northeast, and others.

Summary

Insurers take a number of measures to prevent health insurance fraud and abuse. These include training employees; screening and auditing claims; creating special investigative units; using outside services and databases; and working with insureds, other insurers, government entities, and law enforcement agencies. Insurers also work together in industry associations. Fraud and abuse are usually detected when a claim examiner or claim screening program identifies a characteristic typical of fraud in a claim and passes the claim to an investigator.

Health insurance fraud and abuse and its prevention can be studied in more detail in HIAA's book, *Fraud: The Hidden Cost of Health Care.*

13 PRICING HEALTH INSURANCE PRODUCTS

- *The Four Principles of Insurance Pricing*
- *The Components of a Premium Amount*
- *Claims*
- *Reserves*
- *Margin*
- *Expenses*
- *Profit*
- *Investment Income*

Introduction

In exchange for the protection that an insurance policy provides, the policyholder pays the insurer a premium. The amount of this premium is the price of the policy, and setting the premium amount is known as pricing. Pricing a policy is a complex process in which many factors are taken into account in order to set a premium amount that both makes the policy advantageous and attractive to the insured and also enables the insurer to cover its costs and make a profit (for stock companies) or add to surplus (for mutual companies).

Pricing is done by actuaries (insurance mathematicians) and underwriters. Generally, actuaries establish an insurer's pricing formulas, and underwriters apply these formulas to particular cases.

This chapter explains the principles of pricing and the factors that determine the price of a product. The following chapter describes the pricing process.

The Four Principles of Insurance Pricing

There are four principles that an insurer must follow in setting the amount of a premium:

- **Adequacy.** The amount of the premium for any policy must be adequate to cover the benefit payments the insurer makes on the policy and the costs of administering the policy. For a stock company, the premium must also provide a reasonable amount of profit. For a mutual company, it must also provide a contribution to the surplus the company needs to guarantee its obligations and to fund growth and development. If an insurance company's premiums are not adequate, the company will not be able to meet its costs, it will not be able to make a profit or add to surplus, and it will eventually go out of business.
- **Reasonableness.** Premium amounts must be reasonable in relation to the coverage provided. In other words, people must feel that the coverage they get from a policy is worth the premiums they pay for it. If an insurer charges too much for its coverages, few people will buy them and the insurer could go out of business.
- **Competitiveness.** The premium an insurer charges for a coverage must not be significantly higher than the premiums charged by other insurers for the same coverage. If an insurer charges more than its competitors, few people will buy its policies and it could go out of business. (Competitiveness is similar to reasonableness in that they both relate to what consumers consider a "good price." However, there is a difference: a price is *reasonable* if it is a good price in terms of the benefits it buys; a price is *competitive* if it is a good price compared to the prices of similar products offered by others.)
- **Equity.** Some insureds make more claims than others, and consequently the cost of providing coverage is different for different insureds. The premium amount each insured pays must reflect the expected cost of providing coverage to *that* insured. Why? Suppose an insurer charged some insureds less than the expected cost of providing coverage to them. That insurer would have to charge other insureds an extra amount to make up for those paying less than cost. Those insureds paying extra would go to other insurers that would not charge them extra. The original insurer would be left only with insureds paying less than costs and could go out of business. (Of course, it is impossible to predict precisely what the cost of providing coverage to any insured will be, and consequently premium amounts cannot exactly reflect actual costs, but insurers must strive for equity to the extent possible.)

The Components of a Premium Amount

The principle of adequacy requires that a premium amount be sufficient to cover costs and provide a profit. Therefore, the amount of a premium is based on the estimated amounts of different kinds of costs, plus profit. Thus, profit and the main types of costs can be thought of as components that added together make up the necessary amount of a premium. The cost components are:

- claims (benefit payments);
- reserves (outstanding and future benefit payments, explained below);
- margin (an amount included to cover an unexpectedly large amount of benefit payments); and
- expenses (operational and administrative costs).

Another component is investment income, the revenue that insurers derive from investing the premium payments they receive. Investment income is not added but rather *subtracted* from the necessary amount of a premium, since it is not a cost that the premium must cover but rather a financial gain that partially offsets the need for premium payments.

The way in which these components are combined to arrive at the premium amount can be expressed as a formula:

$$\text{Claims} + \text{Reserves} + \text{Margin} + \text{Expenses} + \text{Profit} - \text{Investment Income} = \text{Premium Amount}$$

In the remainder of this chapter we examine in more detail each of these components.

Claims

The largest cost component of a premium is claims—that is, the cost of paying benefits to insureds covered by the policy. Therefore, a major part of pricing is estimating the total amount of benefit payments that the insurer will make on the policy.

There are two major factors that determine this amount:

- What kinds of losses must the insurer pay benefits for and what amounts must it pay for various losses? This is established by the provisions of the policy.
- How often will insureds incur covered losses and how severe will those losses be? This depends on the morbidity of the people insured.

Morbidity

The term "morbidity" is commonly used to mean simply the likelihood of injury or illness. However, it also has a specific, technical meaning. It is a number that expresses the amount of financial loss that a certain group of people is likely to incur over a certain period of time. (The group of people in question can be the group covered by a group policy or simply the population of all individuals with similar characteristics, such as those of the same age and sex.)

Morbidity is derived by multiplying two other numbers: frequency and severity.

- **Frequency** is how often a loss occurs during a year, expressed as a percentage. For example, if there are normally three hospitalizations for every 100 individuals in a group during a year, the frequency of hospitalization for the group is 3 percent.
- **Severity** is the average amount of loss. To continue the same example, if, when an individual in the group is hospitalized, the cost averages $2,400, the severity of this loss is $2,400.

In this example, the frequency (3 percent) multiplied by the severity ($2,400) gives a morbidity figure for hospitalization for this group of $72. This is the amount of loss per individual per year for hospitalization.

Factors in Morbidity

The morbidity of a group of people depends on the characteristics of those people. Relevant characteristics include the following:

- **Age.** As would be expected, older people have more frequent and more serious health problems than younger people.
- **Sex.** At most ages, women have more health problems on average than men.
- **Income.** Higher-income people tend to seek medical care more frequently and use more services than lower-income people. Also, the amount of disability income benefits is directly based on the income level of the insured.
- **Industry.** Those working in some industries have more frequent and more serious injuries than those in other fields and more frequent and longer periods of disability.
- **Geographic location.** Although the frequency or seriousness of illness and injury does not usually vary by region, the cost of medical treatment does, and this affects the severity amount.

There is an additional morbidity factor in group insurance—the **level of participation** of a group (the percentage of the eligible members of a group who take coverage). When participation is low, there is a greater chance of adverse selection—that is, a greater likelihood that people with health problems will disproportionately choose coverage and make the morbidity of the group higher than it would normally be.

Individual insurance also has an additional factor—whether an individual insured was underwritten and how thoroughly this was done. In some cases, underwriting an individual is prohibited by law, and adverse selection often occurs, making morbidity higher than average. In other cases, underwriting is very thorough, so that any current serious illness is detected, making morbidity lower than average during the first years of the policy.

Reserves

Often an actuary estimates the future claims of an insured group based on the group's past claims during a certain period of time. In taking this approach, the actuary must base her calculation on the number of claims *incurred* during the period of study, which is not the same as the number of claims *paid* during that period. These numbers are not the same because a claim is paid some time after a loss occurs, so that for any period there are always a significant number of claims that were incurred during the period but not paid until later. These are known as **outstanding claims.**

To account for outstanding claims, an actuary includes a **claim reserve** in her calculations. This is an amount to cover the estimated amount of outstanding claims.

There are two types of claim reserves:

* A **pending claim reserve** is for claims that have been made, but that are being processed and have not yet been paid.
* An **incurred but not reported (IBNR) claim reserve** is for losses that insureds have incurred but for which they have not yet submitted claims.

In some cases, future claims as well as outstanding claims must be accounted for. Another type of reserve, known as a policy reserve, is used for this purpose. This will be explained in the following chapter.

Margin

Predictions of future claim levels are usually reasonably accurate, but it does sometimes happen that actual claims are significantly higher than projected. Actuaries add an extra amount to the premium as a protection against this possibility. This amount is known as a **contingency margin** or a **morbidity fluctuation margin**.

The amount of margin needed varies with the likelihood that claims will go above projections. This likelihood depends on a number of factors:

* If the information on which claim projections are based is limited or not considered completely reliable, unexpectedly high claims are more probable and the amount of margin must be greater.

- In group insurance, the larger the group, the smaller the fluctuation in claims and the less likely are unexpectedly high claims. Thus, the larger the group, the smaller the margin.
- Different policies guarantee premium rates for different lengths of time. Underwriters must project claims for the length of time that premiums will stay the same, and the longer that period is, the more difficult accurate prediction is. Therefore, the longer premiums are guaranteed, the greater the margin must be.

Expenses

So far, we have examined claim payments, reserves for outstanding claim payments, and a margin for unexpected claim payments. All costs not related to the money used to pay claims are referred to as expenses and are usually divided into five categories:

- **Sales expenses** are costs associated with the solicitation of new business. The principal cost in this area is sales commissions to agents and brokers, and for this reason sales expenses are sometimes referred to as **sales compensation expenses**. However, other costs fall into this category as well—for example, some companies include the cost of advertising.
- **Acquisition expenses** are costs related to the underwriting, issuance, and installation of policies.
- **Maintenance expenses** are the costs of administering a policy and processing claims. This includes maintaining records, billing and collecting premiums, processing claims, and other activities.
- **General overhead expenses** are the costs of running any business, including the costs of physical plant, office furniture and equipment, recruiting and training, and the salaries of executives.
- **Taxes** include premium taxes (levied by each state) as well as other general business taxes.

Allocating Expenses

Some of the types of expenses listed above are directly related to a particular policy (a sales commission, for example). Other expenses, such as general overhead and maintenance costs, are not associated with any one policy. However, all expenses that an insurer incurs must be paid for by the premium payments the insurer receives. Therefore, the premium of each policy must cover not only those expenses directly related to that policy but also a share of overall expenses. Determining the amount of expenses that must be covered by a policy and included in the premium amount for that policy is known as allocating expenses to the policy.

There are three main ways of allocating expenses:

- **Per policy.** Some expenses (such as underwriting and issuance) are roughly the same for each policy. Total expenses in these areas are divided equally among all policies.
- **Percentage of premium.** The amount of some expenses (such as sales commissions and premium taxes) is directly determined by the amount of premium charged for a policy. These expenses are allocated to each policy according to the amount of premium.
- **Percentage of claims.** Some companies allocate claim administration expenses according to the amount of claims expected to be paid on a policy.

First-Year Expenses

Expenses are normally higher in the first year of a policy than in later years. This is because acquisition expenses are incurred in the first year; also, if a high-low commission schedule is used or sales bonuses paid, sales expenses are higher in the first year. However, an actuary does not set a higher premium for the first year and a lower premium for later years. Instead, he must set one amount such that first-year expenses are amortized (gradually paid for) over several years.

Profit

In setting premiums, insurers that are stock companies must also add an amount for profit. A company's profits are used in two ways: a portion is paid to the company's stockholders as a return on the money they have invested in the company, and a portion is retained by the company to add to its surplus of funds. This surplus serves to ensure that the company will be able to pay claims and otherwise meet its obligations even during times when the insurer's costs exceed its income. An insurer also draws on its surplus for funds needed for growth and development projects.

Mutual insurance companies are not profit-making enterprises and so do not add an amount for profit in setting premiums. However, a mutual insurer, like a stock company, must maintain a surplus as a guarantee of its obligations and a source of growth and development funds, and so mutual companies do add an amount for addition to this surplus.

What determines the amount of profit that is added in setting a premium? In theory, an insurer can add any amount it wants. In practice, however, profit is limited by the principles of pricing discussed at the beginning of this chapter. If profits are too high, premiums will be higher than consumers consider reasonable for the coverage provided and perhaps higher than the premiums of competitors. Profits may also be limited by regulations requiring that a certain percentage of the money that insurers receive as premium payments be returned to insureds as benefit payments.

Profit and the contingency margin, although they are quite different things, are considered together for some purposes. This is because, depending on the amount of claims that are made on a policy, funds may move from one of these categories to the other. The amount of the contingency margin is intended to cover unexpectedly high claims; if claims are not unusually high, all or some of the margin will not be needed for claim payments and the money can be added to profits. On the other hand, if claims are so high that the contingency margin is not sufficient to cover them, funds must be taken from profits to pay them.

Profit and expenses are also grouped together for certain purposes. This is because together they make up the part of a premium amount that is not returned to insureds in the form of benefits but rather retained by the insurer for its purposes. For this reason, they are referred to together as **retention.**

Investment Income

Insurers maintain reserves of funds to cover claims. They also hold a certain amount of money at any given time in cash flow (that is, money that has been received as premiums but not yet paid as benefits). Cash flow and reserve funds are invested, and the return on this investment is used to pay benefits and expenses. Therefore, in calculating the amount of premium needed to pay benefits and expenses, investment income must be subtracted. The exact amount subtracted depends on the amount of reserve funds and cash flow anticipated and general economic factors that determine the rate of return that the insurer can get on its money.

Summary

The pricing of a health insurance product—that is, the setting of the premium amount for a health insurance policy—involves the consideration of a number of factors:

- the amount that the insurer can expect to pay in claims for the policy, which depends on the provisions of the policy and the morbidity of the insureds;
- claim reserves for outstanding claims;
- a contingency margin to cover an unexpectedly high level of claims;
- the expenses of providing coverage and running a business;

- an amount for profit (or in the case of a mutual insurer, addition to surplus); and
- earnings from investment income.

In addition, if an insurer wishes to stay in business, it must adhere to the four principles of pricing: adequacy, reasonableness, competitiveness, and equity.

14 THE PRICING PROCESS

- *Group Rating Methods*
- *Rating Individual Policies*
- *Rerating*
- *The Regulation of Pricing*

Introduction

In the previous chapter we discussed the principles of health insurance pricing. In this chapter, we look at how these principles are put into practice. That is, we examine the steps and procedures that make up the pricing process. This process is in some ways the same and in some ways different for large group plans, small group plans, and individual policies, and all three types of insurance will be discussed.

A clarification of terms: The words "premium" and "premium rate" are sometimes used interchangeably, but there is a distinction. A premium rate is an amount charged per unit of coverage—for instance, per person for group medical expense coverage, or per dollar amount of benefit for individual disability income insurance. A premium, on the other hand, is the total amount charged the policyholder for coverage. For example, an employer providing a group health plan to its employees is charged a certain amount per covered employee—this is the premium rate. That rate is multiplied by the number of covered employees to obtain the total amount the employer pays for coverage—this is the premium. In individual insurance, the premium rate and the premium are often the same—the amount charged per policy. Note also that the term "rating" is often used in place of "pricing."

Group Rating Methods

Three methods are used to set health insurance premium rates for group plans:

- **Experience rating.** The benefits paid to members of the group in the past (the group's claim experience) are used to project future benefit payments to the group, and the group's premium rates are based on these projections.

- **Manual rating.** The premium rates of the group are based on standard rates from the insurer's rating manual; these standard rates are based on averages of the benefit payments made in the past to many groups.
- **Blended manual/experience rating.** Both rates from the manual and the group's claim experience are considered.

Which rating method is used for a given group? In general, experience rating is used for large groups, manual rating is used for small groups, and the blended approach is taken for some medium-size groups. This is because only a large group has a body of claim experience data large enough to be a reliable basis for the prediction of future claims. The claim data of small groups is not large enough to be used in this way, so actuaries use another large body of data—the averages of the claim experience of many groups, contained in the insurer's rating manual. The claim experience of medium-size groups is large enough to be somewhat but not completely reliable, so both manual rates and experience are used.

The type of coverage is also a factor in whether there is a large enough body of claim data for experience rating. Some coverages involve many claims and consequently produce a large body of data, while for other coverages claims are relatively infrequent. For example, a group that has a large number of medical expense insurance claims would probably have many fewer disability income insurance claims, due to the nature of the two coverages. Consequently, a group might be experience-rated for medical expense coverage but manual rated for disability income insurance.

Experience Rating

As explained above, in experience rating, the actuary uses the past claims of the group in question to project the group's future claims and bases premium rates on these projections. The first step in determining the level of past claims is choosing a sample period of time, known as the **experience period**. A period of at least 12 months is normally used to eliminate the normal seasonal variations in illness. The most recent 12-month period has the advantage of reflecting any recent changes that may affect future claim levels. On the other hand, a single year may not be typical, so many insurers use the last several years instead. Some insurers combine both approaches by using several years but giving more weight to recent experience.

After choosing the experience period, the actuary ascertains the amount of the group's incurred claims during that period. As explained in the previous chapter, incurred claims for a period are not the same as the claims the insurer paid during that period. Incurred claims for a given period are all claims paid during the period, *minus* claims paid during the period but incurred before the period began, *plus* estimated amounts (claim reserves) for covered losses that occurred during the period for which claims have not yet been submitted, or for which claims have been submitted but not yet paid.

Once the amount of incurred claims for the experience period has been determined, the actuary uses that amount to project future claims. In general, it is assumed that the amount of past claims is the best predictor of the amount of future claims. However, adjustments are sometimes made to reflect changes that have occurred recently. These may include changes in group characteristics (such as age and income), in health care costs, and in the general business environment (which may affect expenses and investment income). In addition, if any modifications are being made in the benefits provided to the group, these must be taken into account.

When the projection of future claims is finalized, the actuary adds amounts for the other components of a premium that were discussed in the previous chapter—contingency margin, expenses, and profit. Investment income is subtracted.

The result of these calculations is the premium rate (or rates) of a group plan. As explained in the introduction to this chapter, to determine the actual amount of the premium paid by the group policyholder each month, the rate is multiplied by the number of persons covered under that rate.

Manual Rating

Insurers in the small group market create rating manuals for each coverage they sell. The rates of a rating manual are based on the average claim experience of a large number of groups with that coverage. Some insurers have provided this coverage extensively and so have enough claim data from their own groups to produce a manual. Other insurers must use intercompany studies, which contain data from groups of many insurers. Intercompany studies are produced by the Society of Actuaries, other professional organizations, and private consulting firms.

A rating manual contains a range of possible premium rates for a certain coverage. The rates differ according to different benefits provisions and different group characteristics (such as age, sex, geographic location, income, and industry). Manual rating involves matching the benefit package being offered and the characteristics of the group being insured to the proper rate.

The rates in rating manuals are based on claim costs only. The other components of a premium amount (expenses, margin, etc.) involve so many variables that it would be very difficult to incorporate them into manuals. Therefore, actuaries must adjust manual rates to reflect these other components. For example, rates are often increased for smaller groups and decreased for larger ones to reflect the fact that smaller groups have higher expenses per insured person. Profit amounts and contingency margins are also set higher or lower for various reasons.

Blended Manual/Experience Rating

Sometimes a group's body of claim experience data is not large enough for full experience rating, but it is believed that taking the group's past claims into account will make the estimate of future claims more accurate. In such cases, an actuary may blend actual experience with manual rates. This is done in the following way: The **credibility** (reliability) of the group's experience is evaluated and quantified as a percentage. This percentage determines the extent to which experience is used in projecting claim costs. For example, if a group is almost large enough to be fully experience-rated, it might be assigned a credibility percentage of 80, so that the projection of claims would be based 80 percent on the group's experience and 20 percent on manual rates. On the other hand, a smaller group might have a credibility percentage of 30, meaning that only 30 percent of claim projection would be based on experience and 70 percent would be based on the rating manual.

Rating Individual Policies

Individual pricing is similar to small group pricing. Insurers create rating manuals for each coverage, containing premium rates based on the claim experience of a large number of individuals with the same or a similar policy. An insurer may use its own data to create a manual, or it may rely on intercompany studies supplied by the Society of Actuaries or by consultants. Actuaries usually match the benefits provided to an insured and the insured's characteristics (age, sex, occupation, etc.) to the proper premium in the manual and make adjustments for the other premium components.

In some cases, insurers do not set the rates of individual policies according to the characteristics of insureds. Instead they use the same premium rates for all policies providing the same coverage—that is, rates are the same for all persons, regardless of such characteristics as age, sex, and occupation. This is known as **community rating** and is sometimes required by state insurance law.

Rating for Aging in Individual Policies

Morbidity normally increases with age. This means that in an individual policy, the level of claims almost always increases during the life of the policy, as the insured ages. (Group policies do not usually have this problem, because as older workers retire and younger workers are hired, the average age of the group tends to remain relatively stable.) There are two ways to address the problem:

• Rates can be set to go up automatically as the insured ages. This is known as **attained-age rating**. Rates may increase each year or only when the insured moves from one age band to another. (Age bands are groupings such as 20 to 29 years old, 30 to 39, and so forth.)

- Rates do not go up with age. In this approach, **level rating**, rates are set such that during the early years of the policy the insurer makes more than enough to cover costs. This extra money is put into a reserve (known as a **policy reserve** or **active life reserve**) and invested, and the earnings are used to pay benefits in the later years of the policy, when claims exceed premiums.

A common form of level rating is **entry-age rating**. In this system, rates do not go up with age, but an individual's rate depends in part on her age when she first bought the policy—those who buy when they are young get better rates than those who buy when they are older. This encourages people to begin coverage at a younger age.

Level rating is complex, as rates must be set such that claims and premiums balance out over a long period of time. Attained-age rating is less complicated, simply involving applying the overall morbidity rates of different age groups, but it has a different problem—continually rising rates tend to discourage insureds from continuing coverage.

Rerating

The pricing of a health insurance product does not end with the setting of the initial premium rate. For medical expense coverage and most group coverages, initial rates are usually guaranteed for 12 months (sometimes longer), but after that time the insurer may change rates, either at set intervals or on any premium due date. Resetting rates is called rerating. Rerating is most commonly done on an annual basis, with rates changing on the anniversary of the effective date of the policy.

The rerating process is essentially the same as that of rating—that is, actuaries try to predict the future level of claims and other costs and set premium rates that will cover these costs and provide a profit while keeping the policy competitive. However, rerating differs somewhat in that actuaries do not start at zero in making predictions, but rather review the projections of claims and expenses made in setting rates previously and compare those projections to actual experience. Actuaries also often make an in-depth analysis of the claims of a group or a category of individual policies in an effort to identify emerging trends that might affect future claim levels.

Rerating can take several weeks to several months, and an insurer must usually give a policyholder at least 30 days' notice of any rate change. Consequently, rerating must begin well in advance of the rate change date. Because of this, when an insurer is rerating at the end of the first year of coverage, it must make a choice. If the insurer wants a rate change to be effective on the first anniversary date, rerating must begin a few months before that date and will be based on less than a year's claim experience (often nine months). On the other hand, if the insurer wants to base rerating on a full year of claim experience, it must defer a rate change until three or four months after the anniversary date. A full year's claim experience is more reliable and an insurer usually prefers to rerate on that basis, but if there are indications that claims are higher than expected, the insurer may feel that it cannot wait to increase rates.

If the rerating process shows that a rate increase is needed for a policy, the insurer may offer the policyholder an alternative. For example, the insurer may suggest a reduction in benefits that will reduce claims and make the rate increase unnecessary. Claims can also be reduced by an increase in deductibles or coinsurance or the introduction of managed care features.

Insurers can also avoid rate increases by allowing one coverage to subsidize another. Normally, when an insurer provides a package of several coverages to an individual or group, the coverages do not subsidize one another—that is, not only does the whole package produce a profit, but so does each separate coverage. In rerating, however, one coverage is sometimes allowed to pay for another in order to avoid a price increase. For example, an insurer may be earning very little profit on the disability income insurance of a group health plan but a greater than expected profit on the plan's medical expense coverage. As long as the whole plan is profitable, the insurer may decide not to raise rates on any coverage.

Experience Refunds

Some large group policies have a provision requiring experience refunds. This means that if the cost of providing coverage turns out to be less than the insurer projected, the insurer must refund a portion of premium payments to the policyholder. Rerating and experience refund determination are normally done together, as they both involve examining actual claim experience and comparing it to the claim level that was projected. However, it must be kept in mind that the two processes have different goals. Rerating analyzes recent claim experience in order to more accurately project future claims; the experience refund determination process, on the other hand, looks for divergences between claims for a recent period and the projections made for that period so that the difference can be reimbursed to the policyholder.

The Regulation of Pricing

The pricing process is subject to a number of state laws and regulations.

- Insurers often must submit premium rates to state insurance departments for review and approval.
- Most states use minimum loss ratio standards to evaluate premiums for individual policies. A **loss ratio** is the proportion of premium payments that is returned to insureds in the form of benefit payments.
- Some states have **mandated benefits**—that is, they require all policies of a certain type to cover certain medical services. These mandates can result in additional claims and administrative costs that must be reflected in the premium rate.
- Some states prohibit or limit basing premium rates for individuals on an individual's age, sex, or occupation.
- Several states have enacted **small group reform legislation**, which regulates pricing and other aspects of health insurance policies for groups of two to 25 (or sometimes two to 50) full-time permanent employees. Insurers can charge different rates to different groups in this category according to group characteristics, but only within certain limits. (For example, in many states, no group may be charged a rate more than 25 percent greater than the average rate.) Most states also limit the amount of rate increases for these groups. In addition, no individual member of these groups can be charged a different premium rate based on her medical history.

Summary

The largest component in the amount of a health insurance premium is claim costs. Therefore, the most important part of the process of pricing a policy is predicting the amount of claim payments that the insurer will make on the policy. For large groups, this prediction is usually based on the past claims of the group. For small groups and individuals, averages of the claims of other groups and individuals, contained in rating manuals, are generally used. For some medium-size groups, a mixed approach is taken.

Once the level of claims is projected, the other components of the premium amount are calculated and the premium set. If the policy continues after its initial term, rates will have to be reevaluated periodically.

15 THE REGULATION OF INSURANCE

- **Why Is Insurance Regulated?**
- **The Regulatory Environment of Insurance**

- **Insurer Compliance with Laws and Regulations**

Introduction

In this book and in the preceding book in this series, *The Health Insurance Primer*, we have looked at all the major aspects of health insurance: the different kinds of coverage, the contract, sales and marketing, underwriting, administration, claims, cost control, fraud, and pricing. In almost every chapter, relevant laws and government regulations are discussed. This is a reflection of the importance of regulation in every area of health insurance.

It is also a result of our approach to explaining regulation. Rather than listing and describing all important laws and regulations in one place, we have chosen to present each law within the context of the area of health insurance that the law relates to. (Some laws, notably HIPAA, impact several areas and so appear in several chapters.) We believe this method leads to a better understanding of the many ways in which health insurance is affected by regulation.

Since specific laws and regulations have already been discussed in previous chapters, they are not the main focus of our chapters on regulation. Instead, a general overview of health insurance regulation is presented. This chapter discusses why insurance (both health insurance and other kinds of coverage) is regulated and describes the regulatory environment, including the different kinds of regulation and the roles of the different levels and branches of government. Chapter 16 summarizes the kinds of health insurance regulations imposed by state governments and explains how those regulations are administered and enforced by states. Chapter 17 reviews federal laws and federal government programs that have an impact on the health insurance industry.

Why Is Insurance Regulated?

Of course, all sectors of the economy are subject to some government regulation. But regulation of the insurance industry is particularly extensive. Why is this? There are two important issues that arise in insurance of any type that have created a demand for greater regulation of this field:

- **Solvency.** In most business transactions, one party pays money to another party and in return receives a good or service from that party. An insurance transaction is somewhat different. The policyholder pays premiums to the insurer, and what she receives in return is the insurer's promise that if she suffers a covered loss, the insurer will pay her a benefit. However, for this promise to be worth anything, the policyholder must be reasonably sure that the insurer will have sufficient funds to meet its future obligations, including the payment of benefits—that is, it must be reasonably certain that the insurer will be solvent. Policyholders do not normally have the resources and skills needed to ascertain whether an insurer is and will continue to be solvent. Therefore, government regulators have taken responsibility for verifying and ensuring the solvency of insurers.
- **Contracts.** Insurance contracts are highly technical documents. Of course, this is true of many kinds of contracts, but what makes insurance contracts different is that while one party to the contract, the insurer, has expertise in these contracts, the other party, the policyholder, usually does not. That is, while insurer person-nel have the knowledge needed to completely understand all of the provisions of an insurance contract and their implications, the policyholder does not have this knowledge and so cannot determine if a contract is reasonable and fair. (This is especially true for individual insurance, where the policyholder is a private citizen rather than a business.) As a result, governments act to protect the interests of policyholders by establishing standards of fairness and requiring that all insurance contracts meet them.

Neither of these issues is unique to insurance. Solvency is a concern for all **fidu-ciary organizations** (businesses such as insurers, banks, and trust companies that hold money in trust for others). And average consumers enter into technical contracts that they do not have the expertise to fully understand in other fields such as real estate. But the regulations intended to address these two issues, plus the regulations that all businesses are subject to (such as those governing truth in advertising, confidentiality of personal information, discrimination, and taxation), add up to a high degree of regulation for the insurance industry.

The Regulatory Environment of Insurance

Insurance of all kinds is governed by state and federal laws and regulations and by court interpretations of these laws and regulations. In this section, we look at each of these elements of the regulatory environment of insurance.

The Roles of State Governments and the Federal Government

State governments began enacting laws related to insurance in the 19th century, and by the early 20th century, state insurance regulation was extensive. Then in 1944, the U.S. Supreme Court ruled that insurance is interstate commerce, which the Constitution gives the federal government the right to regulate. Thus Congress, not the states, has the right to make insurance laws. However, in the McCarran-Ferguson Act of 1945, Congress decided to grant this right to the states and allow the states to continue regulating insurance. But Congress did not give up the right to legislate in this area and, while it has allowed states to take the principal role in insurance regulation, it has enacted laws affecting insurance. As a result, the insurance industry is regulated primarily by the states, but it is also impacted by federal laws and regulations. In recent years, Congress has legislated more in this area, and consequently the federal role has increased in importance.

State Laws and Regulations

The legislature of each state enacts laws governing insurance in that state. In most states, insurance laws are grouped together in what is known as the **insurance code**. An agency of the executive branch of each state government, usually the **state insurance department**, has the responsibility of administering and enforcing the insurance laws passed by the legislature. To better perform this function, these departments draft and issue rules that specify what insurers, agents, and others must do to comply with the laws. These rules are known as **official regulations**. In addition, insurance departments publish bulletins, guidelines, and official letters that clarify laws and official regulations, and these documents are sometimes referred to as **informal regulations** or **regulatory guidance.**

Thus, we can draw a distinction between laws and regulations—laws are enacted by a legislature and regulations are issued by a government agency. However, in practice the word "regulation" is often used to refer to all government rules, including both laws and regulations.

State insurance departments, in addition to issuing regulations, perform many other functions in the fulfillment of their mission of administering and enforcing insurance laws. These functions include licensing insurers and agents; examining insurers; and reviewing policies, premium rates, and insurer financial reports. The operations of state insurance departments will be discussed in the following chapter.

Differences and Similarities among State Laws and Regulations

Since the legislature of each state enacts the insurance laws for that state, and each state insurance department issues its own regulations, laws and regulations of course vary from state to state. However, the National Association of Insurance Commissioners (NAIC), made up of the heads of the state insurance departments, works to bring about greater uniformity. The NAIC does this by developing model laws and regulations to address various issues and problems and recommending that all states adopt them. When the NAIC proposes a model law, some state legislatures may enact it without change and others may adopt modified versions of it or adopt it in part. Still other states may not adopt a model law at all. In general, however, the laws of all states have been influenced to some degree by NAIC models. As a result, there are both differences and similarities in the laws and regulations of the states.

The balance between laws and regulations also varies from state to state. In some states, there are only a few laws that establish general principles and most specific issues are dealt with by regulations. Other states have a comprehensive body of insurance laws that address most issues that arise, so that regulations are less important. Thus, while one state may have more insurance laws than another, this does not necessarily mean that the regulation of insurance is stricter in the first state. The second state may have few laws but extensive regulations.

The Scope of State Laws

Usually, a state's insurance laws apply only to policies issued in that state. In other words, if an insurance company whose main operations are in State A sells a policy to a resident of State B, that policy is subject to the laws of State A but is usually not subject to the laws of State B.

However, a number of states have some laws that are **extraterritorial**. These laws apply to policies issued in other states that cover residents of the state. In other words, suppose (as in the above example) that a company headquartered in State A sells a policy to a resident of State B. As noted, normally this policy is subject to the laws of State A, not those of State B. However, if State B has any extraterritorial laws the policy is subject to those laws as well as all the laws of State A. Obviously, extraterritorial laws make complying with regulations more complicated, as a policy may have to meet the requirements of two or more states.

Federal Laws and Regulations

As noted above, the U.S. Congress, while allowing the states to continue to take the primary role in regulating insurance, reserves the right to make laws affecting insurance and does, in fact, enact such laws from time to time. Federal insurance laws are administered and enforced by various agencies of the executive branch of the federal government, and these agencies may also issue insurance regulations.

Judicial Interpretation

We have seen that at both the state and federal levels, the legislative and executive branches of government are involved in regulating insurance—the legislature enacts laws and the executive branch administers those laws and issues regulations based on them. The judicial branch also plays a role. Courts often hear lawsuits in which an insurance law or regulation or the language of an insurance contract is an important factor. In such cases, a court may have to decide precisely what actions are permitted and forbidden by a law or regulation, or whether a regulation issued by a government agency is consistent with relevant laws, or what the language of a contract means. Such decisions create judicial precedents that determine how laws and regulations are applied and how contracts are interpreted. In this way, judicial action influences and shapes the body of laws and regulations that governs insurance.

Insurer Compliance with Laws and Regulations

Insurance company personnel must take steps to ensure that the company fulfills the requirements of all state and federal laws and regulations. This area of activity is referred to as **regulatory compliance**. Compliance involves reviewing the practices and actions of all company departments. It also entails monitoring changes in the regulatory environment (such as new laws, regulations, and court decisions), deciding how to adapt to those changes, and implementing new practices.

In different insurance companies, different entities have the responsibility for regulatory compliance:

- Some insurers have a **compliance committee**. This committee is composed of representatives of various areas of the company and meets on a regular basis to discuss compliance issues and recommend action.
- Other insurers hire a person or staff of persons to handle compliance. If this staff is large, it is called a **compliance division**. Compliance divisions are typical of larger companies for whom compliance is complex because they operate in many states and sell a variety of coverages.

An insurance company's legal department also plays a role in compliance. It renders opinions on the meaning of laws, regulations, or court decisions. In some companies, it has the responsibility of keeping informed of changes in regulation.

National insurance industry associations such as the Health Insurance Association of America (HIAA) assist insurers in the area of compliance. They follow developments in legislation, regulation, and the courts at the state and federal levels and publish bulletins informing insurers of possible or actual changes.

Summary

Businesses of all kinds are subject to government regulation, but the regulation of insurance is more extensive, due primarily to the issues of solvency and contracts. Insurance is regulated primarily by the states, but is also governed by federal laws and regulations. Each state enacts its own insurance laws. These laws are administered and enforced by state insurance departments, which issue regulations specifying how laws are to be complied with. Laws and regulations vary from state to state, but there is some degree of similarity as a result of the adoption (with or without modifications) of NAIC model laws by many states. Judicial decisions are another element in the regulatory environment—they influence how insurance laws, regulations, and contracts are interpreted and applied. Insurance companies must take measures to ensure that they are following all laws and regulations—this area of activity is known as regulatory compliance.

16 STATE REGULATION OF HEALTH INSURANCE

- *Areas Addressed by State Health Insurance Laws and Regulations*
- *Administering and Enforcing State Insurance Laws: The State Insurance Department*
- *State Taxes and Fees*

Introduction

We saw in the previous chapter that insurance is a highly regulated industry, due to concerns about solvency and contracts. In the health insurance field, additional issues arise, such as availability and affordability of coverage. This chapter examines how state regulations address these matters.

Because of the differences from state to state, we do not discuss specific laws, regulations, and practices. Instead, we address two general questions:

- What aspects of health insurance do state governments regulate, and what kinds of laws and regulations do they establish?
- How do state insurance departments administer and enforce state laws and regulations?

Areas Addressed by State Health Insurance Laws and Regulations

Policy Provisions

Some state health insurance laws and regulations require that all policies (or all policies of a certain kind) contain certain provisions. State laws and regulations also forbid certain provisions. There are many such laws, and they address a wide range of issues. We have discussed some of the most common policy provision requirements and prohibitions in this book and *The Health Insurance Primer*. To give just a few examples, we saw that laws require provisions that give policyholders certain rights of renewal or reinstatement, provisions that limit the insurer's right to contest a policy, and provisions that provide benefits for certain expenses (such as mental health services).

Required benefit provisions are known as **mandated benefits** or **mandates** and are becoming more common. Moreover, while in the past mandates generally pertained only to group insurance, increasingly they apply to individual policies as well.

Solvency

As explained in the previous chapter, one of the principal reasons that insurance is regulated is to make sure insurance companies have the financial resources to pay claims and otherwise meet their financial obligations. State laws seek to do this in two main ways:

- They require insurers to have a certain amount of financial reserves.
- They restrict the investments insurers can make. Typically, state laws require a diversification of investments and limit investments that tend to fluctuate greatly in value.

State laws also require insurers to report financial information to the states. (Financial reporting is discussed later in this chapter.)

Claim Administration

Most states have laws and regulations governing insurers' handling of claims. Insurers may not:

- misrepresent the facts of a case or the provisions of a policy;
- refuse to pay a claim without conducting a reasonable investigation based on all available information;
- refuse to explain the reason for denying a claim; or
- force the insured to start legal action to collect an amount due.

In addition, the laws of many states establish time limits within which the insurer must acknowledge a claim, furnish claim forms, answer a claimant's correspondence, and pay or deny a claim. In an increasing number of states, the insurer must pay the claimant interest on amounts that are due but not paid within a specified number of days.

Other Areas Regulated

- **Premium rates.** As we saw in Chapter 14, many states restrict pricing in various ways. This usually includes requiring a certain balance between the benefits provided by a policy and the premiums charged.

- **The availability of coverage.** Some state laws are intended to increase the availability of health insurance. A common approach is mandating **guaranteed issue**—that is, requiring any insurer selling to a certain market (for example, small groups) to accept any applicant that meets certain basic eligibility requirements.
- **Agents and brokers.** States require insurance agents and brokers to have licenses, and they regulate the conduct of agents and brokers in various ways.
- **Advertising.** State laws require that all advertising relating to health insurance be truthful and not misleading in fact or by implication. Deceptive words, phrases, or illustrations are prohibited. Statistics used in ads must be relevant, and their sources must be identified. Exceptions and limitations must be clearly set forth, including those relating to preexisting conditions. Advertisements must disclose policy provisions relating to renewability, cancelability, and termination.
- **Readability.** Some state laws require the language of a policy to be understandable by the average consumer. Objective readability tests, based on the length of words and sentences, are sometimes applied.
- **Personal information.** Laws establish standards for the way personal information may be obtained in connection with insurance transactions and how this information can be used and disclosed.
- **Discrimination.** As we will see, federal law prohibits discrimination in health insurance based on ethnicity, religion, sex, or age. The laws of some states also prohibit discrimination based on other criteria, such as marital status, sexual orientation, deafness, blindness, visual acuity, lawful occupation, or the presence of certain genetic traits (most commonly sickle cell and Tay-Sachs diseases).

Group and Individual Insurance

Both group and individual health insurance are subject to regulation in the areas listed above. However, the specific laws and regulations that apply to individual and group policies often differ to reflect differences in the two types of insurance. It should also be noted that there are some types of regulations that by their nature pertain only to either group or individual insurance. Examples include laws that establish what groups are eligible for group insurance or set minimum enrollment requirements for groups.

Administering and Enforcing State Insurance Laws: The State Insurance Department

As noted in the previous chapter, every state government has a department with the responsibility of administering and enforcing the state's insurance laws. Usually, this is the state insurance department; in a few states, there is one department that handles the regulation of both insurance and banking, or one department for all business regulation. The head of a state insurance department is usually called the **insurance commissioner** (sometimes the insurance superintendent or director). The commissioner is most often appointed by the governor and confirmed by the legislature, but she may be elected. The commissioner reports to the governor, but the legislature, in addition to enacting the laws that the insurance department enforces and that govern its operation, controls the department's budget.

To fulfill its mission of administering and enforcing the state's insurance laws, the insurance department engages in a number of activities, described below.

Licensing Insurers and Agents

The laws of most states establish that no insurance company may do business in the state without a license to do so from that state. This license is granted by the state insurance department. This prerogative gives the insurance department great power in enforcing laws and regulations—if the department determines that an insurer's operations are not in compliance with the law or are in some other way unsatisfactory (as when the company's solvency is questionable), the department can withhold or withdraw the insurer's license, and the insurer will not be able to sell insurance in the state.

State laws also establish that no insurance agent (or broker) may sell policies in the state without a license to do so, and these licenses are also granted by the state insurance department. As with insurers, the licensing of agents gives the department strong enforcement powers—if an agent does not comply with the laws and regulations of the state, her license can be withdrawn, and she will not be able to sell policies in the state.

To obtain an insurance agent's license, a person must pass a written examination, or, in some states, she must complete an approved course of study. Licenses are sometimes permanent, but more often they must be renewed annually. Most states require as a condition of renewal that agents submit proof of having earned continuing education units (CEUs). Agents also usually pay an annual license fee.

Reviewing Policies and Rates

The laws of most states require that before an insurer issues any insurance policy in the state, it must submit that policy to the state insurance department for prior approval. The act of submitting a policy for approval by the insurance department is known as **filing the policy**. Filing is required so that regulators can verify the following:

- The policy complies with all state laws and regulations.
- The terms of the policy are fair to the insured.
- The language of the policy is clear, unambiguous, consistent, and not misleading in any way.

If a policy does not meet these requirements, the insurance department will not approve it and it cannot be used in the state.

In addition, most states require insurers to file some premium rates. The purpose of this requirement is to enable the insurance department to confirm that the premium charged is reasonable in relation to the benefits provided.

The requirements for the filing of premium rates vary from state to state and differ for individual and group insurance. Most states require insurers to file all rates for individual health insurance policies. Some states also require insurers to file their standard first-year group rates from their rating manuals.

Premium rate filing requirements also differ according to when the insurer can begin charging the rate. In some cases, insurers must "file for approval"—that is, they cannot charge the rate until it has been approved. In other cases, insurers can "file and use"—they can begin charging the rate as soon as they have filed it, without waiting for approval.

For both group and individual health insurance, some states require an actuarial memorandum showing how rates were developed and indicating the anticipated loss ratio (the proportion of premium payments returned to the insured as benefit payments). For individual insurance, insurers may have to file the actual loss ratios for each year.

Reviewing Insurer Financial Reports and Dealing with Insolvency

The insurance companies licensed by a state are required to submit annual statements to the state insurance department. These statements show the insurer's financial condition and its financial results for the year. They include information on the insurer's assets, liabilities, reserves, surplus, investments, income, operating costs, and other matters. This information is used by the insurance department to confirm that the insurer is solvent—that is, that the insurer has sufficient assets to pay its claims and meet its other obligations.

If an insurance company becomes insolvent or is in danger of doing so, the insurance department has the power to assume control of the company. The department normally makes every attempt to restore the insurer to solvency. If that is impossible, the department liquidates the company. In the liquidation process, the department attempts to find a solvent company to take over the policies of the insolvent insurer.

Examining Insurers

State insurance departments conduct examinations of insurance companies to verify that their practices are in compliance with state laws and regulations and that they are financially stable. In general, insurance departments examine insurers on a periodic basis, usually every three to five years, but additional examinations may occur. Every state insurance department has the right to examine any insurer operating in that state, but in practice the examination of an insurer is usually conducted by the insurance department of the state where it is headquartered, and the other states where the insurer operates accept the results of that examination. However, in some cases, several states collaborate in examining an insurer.

To conduct an examination, insurance department examiners normally visit the insurance company and review in detail the company's operation. Examiners have the right to inspect the company records and to interrogate all officers, agents, and employees. An examination often requires a number of months, even as much as a year for large insurers. The insurer pays for the cost of the examination.

Sometimes only a part of an insurer's operations is examined. A common type of partial examination is a **market conduct examination**. Market conduct examinations focus on how a company behaves toward consumers, looking at its sales and marketing activities, underwriting and rating practices, claim administration, policyholder service, and complaint handling. A market conduct examination may look at all of these areas or target one or a few of them, perhaps in response to complaints against the company.

The findings of an examination are provided to the company in a written report, which may include recommendations for changes in the company's operations. A follow-up examination may be conducted to determine if these recommendations have been followed.

Investigating Complaints

State insurance departments receive and investigate complaints from policyholders and insureds. In many states, insurers must provide the address and telephone number of the state insurance department to insureds in case they want to file a complaint.

Complaints are most common in the areas of claim administration, underwriting, and sales. In claim complaints, insureds usually believe a claim that was denied should have been paid. Underwriting complaints commonly involve a dispute as to the individual's insurability. Improper methods used by an agent are typically the basis for sales complaints.

If an insurance department receives a complaint about an insurer, department personnel first ask the insurer for an explanation. If it appears that the complaint may be valid, the department may require the insurer to provide more information. If a violation of law is found to have occurred, the department can impose penalties. Complaints about agents are handled in essentially the same way.

Imposing Penalties for Noncompliance

As we saw above, if an insurer or agent violates the laws and regulations of a state, the state insurance department has the authority to revoke its license. However, license revocation is considered a very severe penalty. It effectively puts the company or the businessperson out of business in the state and may even lead to the loss of licenses in other states. Consequently, the penalty of revocation is rarely imposed—it is usually used only in very serious cases. Nevertheless, because of its severity, revocation serves as a powerful incentive for compliance.

For most violations, the insurer or agent must pay a fine. The amount of a fine may be small, but for a serious violation it can be quite large. In some cases, an insurer may have to pay multiple fines—for example, if an insurer does not submit a policy for approval prior to issuing it, it may have to pay a fine for every individual covered by that policy.

Insurers and agents have another incentive to make sure they are in compliance with all laws and regulations. If they are found guilty of a violation, they are often subject to closer scrutiny by regulators. Examinations may be done more frequently, and policies and reports may be looked at more carefully. This may occur not only in the state where the violation occurred but in other states as well.

State Taxes and Fees

Regulation is not the only way in which state governments affect the insurance industry. The tax laws of states also have an impact.

States require insurance companies to pay a tax on the premium payments they receive. All states impose a premium tax on insurers headquartered out of the state but operating in the state; some states' premium tax also applies to in-state insurers, although they are usually charged a lower rate than out-of-state insurers.

In addition, states often charge insurers a fee for the privilege of doing business in the state. Fees are also charged for many of the transactions involved in administering insurance regulation, such as licensing insurers and agents and filing policies and financial statements.

Summary

State laws and regulations address the following areas of health insurance:

- policy provisions
- solvency
- claim administration
- premium rates
- availability of coverage
- agents and brokers
- advertising
- readability
- personal information
- discrimination

State insurance departments determine whether insurers and agents are in compliance with state laws and regulations by conducting examinations of insurers, reviewing policies and premium rates, reviewing insurer financial reports, and investigating complaints. If an insurer or agent is found to be in violation, a fine is usually imposed. In very serious cases, licenses may be revoked.

17 FEDERAL GOVERNMENT INVOLVEMENT IN HEALTH INSURANCE

- *Major Federal Legislation Affecting Health Insurance*
- *Federal Health Care Benefit Programs*

Introduction

Although state governments take the primary role in regulating insurance, the federal government is also involved in the health insurance field. This involvement takes two forms:

- Congress enacts laws that affect health insurance.
- Federal government programs provide health care benefits to certain classes of people, and these programs have an impact on the environment in which health insurance companies operate.

Some of these laws and programs have been mentioned or described in previous chapters of this book and *The Health Insurance Primer*. In this final chapter, we provide an overview of federal health insurance legislation and health care benefit programs.

Major Federal Legislation Affecting Health Insurance

The Employee Retirement Income Security Act (ERISA)

The principal purpose of ERISA is to regulate employer-sponsored pension plans in order to protect the interests of employees participating in them. However, ERISA also regulates employer-sponsored benefit plans, including group health insurance plans.

ERISA imposes requirements on employers sponsoring such plans in three main areas:

- **Disclosure and reporting.** An employer sponsoring a benefit plan must give participants a **summary plan description**. This document informs participants of their rights and obligations under the plan. If the plan covers more than 100 persons, the employer must make the summary plan description available on request to the U.S. Department of Labor.
- **Fiduciary responsibility.** The employer must name one or more **fiduciaries** (trustees) of a benefit plan. These are persons who have the authority to manage the operation of the plan and the obligation to act in the interest of the participants.
- **Claims.** When an employee benefit plan denies a participant's claim, it must give an adequate explanation, and the participant must have the right to have his claim reviewed by the plan's fiduciary.

ERISA includes a **preemption provision** stating that, because ERISA imposes federal regulations on employers sponsoring benefit plans, these employers are preempted (exempt) from any state laws intended to regulate their involvement in these plans. There have been many legal challenges to various state laws based on this preemption provision. In general, the courts have upheld the preemption provision and denied states the right to regulate plan sponsors in cases where ERISA applies.

It should be clarified that while ERISA exempts employers from state laws intended to regulate their management of benefit plans, insurers who provide coverage for such plans *are not exempt* from state laws and regulations. Two examples will clarify this distinction: Alpine Corporation is self-insured—that is, it provides its own employee health insurance plan, and no insurance company is involved. Alpine's plan is subject to ERISA but not state laws and regulations governing insurance. Piedmont, Inc., on the other hand, is not self-insured; its employee health insurance plan is provided by Delta Insurance Company. Piedmont's involvement in its plan is subject to ERISA, and in addition Delta's involvement in the plan is subject to state insurance laws and regulations.

The Health Insurance Portability and Accountability Act (HIPAA)

The Health Insurance Portability and Accountability Act was enacted in 1996 with the purpose of expanding access to health insurance. HIPAA represented a major change in the regulatory environment because, although Congress had previously passed laws that affected health insurance in various ways, HIPAA was the first major piece of federal legislation that regulated health insurers. Thus, HIPAA marked a shift away from Congress's previous approach of leaving the regulation of health insurance to the states.

Several of the provisions of HIPAA have already been discussed in various chapters of this book and *The Health Insurance Primer.* The most important of these provisions are the following:

- Insurers selling individual health insurance policies must provide coverage to people who have lost their group coverage because they have changed or lost their jobs, provided certain conditions are met.
- Exclusions of preexisting conditions in group health insurance policies are limited in several ways.
- Insurers selling to the small group market must accept every small group that applies for coverage and must accept every eligible individual in a group, provided she applies when she first becomes eligible.
- Insurers must renew group and individual medical expense insurance policies except in a few specified circumstances.

The Consolidated Omnibus Budget Reconciliation Act (COBRA)

COBRA requires employers with 20 or more employees to allow continuation of group health care coverage for 18 months, at the employee's expense, for employees (and their dependents) who leave the company for any reason other than gross misconduct.

Family and Medical Leave Act (FMLA)

FMLA gives eligible employees the right to take up to 12 work weeks of unpaid leave during a 12-month period for:

- the birth, adoption, or foster care placement of a child;
- a serious health condition that prevents the employee from performing the essential functions of her job; or
- caring for a child, spouse, or parent with a serious health condition.

FMLA affects health insurance because it also requires that while an employee is on family or medical leave, she must continue to be covered by her group health insurance plan.

For more information on HIPAA, COBRA, and FMLA, see *The Health Insurance Primer.*

Employment and Anti-Discrimination Laws

Various federal employment and anti-discrimination laws govern the group health insurance plans employers provide for their employees. Insurers must adhere to these laws in designing, underwriting, and rating group plans.

- **Title Seven of the Civil Rights Act of 1964** prohibits employers from discriminating against any individual on the basis of race, color, religion, sex, or national origin with respect to compensation or the terms, conditions, or privileges of employment—including the right to participate in an employer-sponsored group health insurance plan and the terms of participation in that plan.
- **A 1978 amendment to Title Seven of the Civil Rights Act** requires employers to treat pregnancy, for all employment-related purposes, the same as any other medical condition. This includes the payment of disability income insurance and medical expense insurance benefits. One notable exception to the law is that the employer does not have to provide medical expense benefits for abortions unless a woman's life would be endangered if an abortion is not performed. Employers must also pay benefits for the treatment of any medical complications resulting from an abortion. The law has been interpreted to mean that dependent wives must receive the same pregnancy benefits as female employees.
- **The Age Discrimination in Employment Act (ADEA)** prohibits employers with 20 or more employees from discriminating against individuals aged 40 or older in all aspects of employment, including employee benefits. The law does allow for a reduction in disability benefits for older employees, provided the employer is spending the same amounts on all employees. That is, a lower level of benefits can be provided to older employees if the premium paid is equivalent to the premium paid for a higher level of benefits for younger employees.
- **The Americans with Disabilities Act (ADA)** bans discrimination against disabled people in a number of areas, including employment and employee benefits such as health insurance.

Fair Credit Reporting Act

The Fair Credit Reporting Act regulates organizations involved in gathering, using, and reporting credit, employment, and insurance information on individuals. It requires that such organizations adopt reasonable procedures to ensure the following:

- Information is accurate and current.
- Only relevant information is used.
- Confidentiality is protected.
- Information is used in a way that is proper and fair to individuals.

Federal Health Care Benefit Programs

Medicare

The Medicare program pays benefits for health care expenses of persons aged 65 or older and others with certain disabilities. Medicare benefits are divided into Part A and Part B.

All Medicare beneficiaries receive Part A benefits. Beneficiaries do not pay premiums for Part A, which is financed by payroll deductions paid by employees and employers. Part A pays benefits for hospital care, skilled nursing care, home health services, hospice care, and blood.

Medicare Part B is optional, and those participating must pay a portion of premiums. (The rest of the premium is paid by the government.) Medicare Part B pays benefits for some services not covered by Part A.

Medicare beneficiaries must pay deductibles and coinsurance for both Part A and Part B benefits. (See *The Health Insurance Primer* for more information on the Medicare program.)

The Medicare program and private health insurance interact in many ways. A few examples:

- Some insurers market Medicare supplement insurance, which fills the gaps in the benefits provided by Medicare.
- Many group policies stipulate that dependent coverage for a spouse ends when the spouse becomes eligible for Medicare benefits.
- Federal laws make the Medicare program the secondary payer to employers' group health plans in certain circumstances. This means that the group plan pays benefits first and Medicare pays for expenses not covered by the group plan.

Medicaid

The Medicaid program pays benefits for health care expenses of the poor. Medicaid is a federally sponsored program, but state governments are also involved. Each state provides a set of benefits to the poor and, provided that the benefit package meets certain requirements, the federal government pays a portion of the cost. Federal requirements for state programs include the following:

- Benefits must be available to all those who qualify for public assistance, including families with dependent children and needy persons who are elderly, blind, or disabled. (A state may also include people who do not qualify for public assistance but whom the state determines to be medically needy.)

FIGURE 17.1

Sources of Health Insurance for Nonelderly Americans

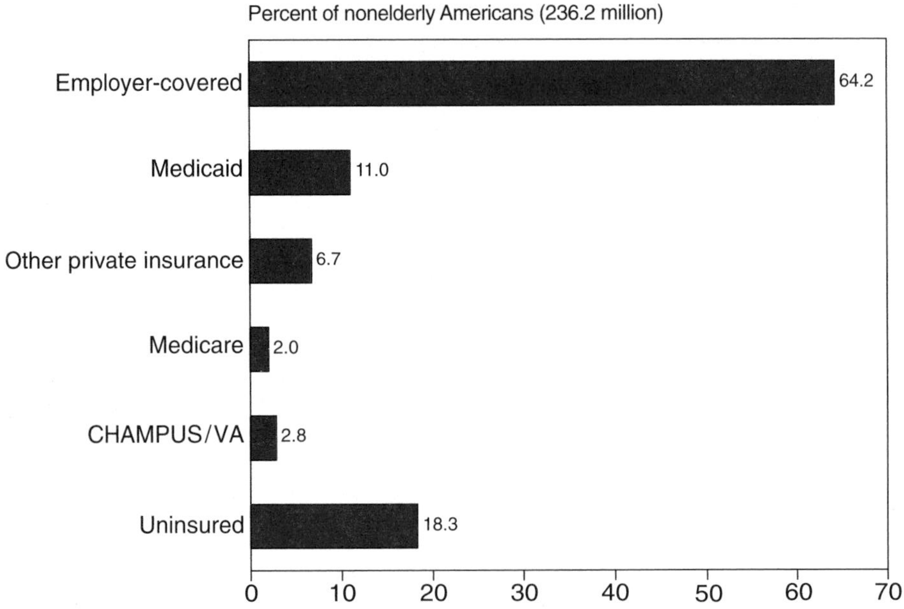

Percent of nonelderly Americans (236.2 million)

Source: Employee Benefit Research Institute, Analysis of March 1998 Current Population Survey.

- A minimal level of benefits must be provided in these areas: inpatient and outpatient hospital care, physicians' services, skilled nursing home care, home health care, laboratory and X-ray services, screening and diagnosis for children under age 21, and family planning.
- The required minimal benefits must be provided without cost sharing (deductibles, coinsurance, or copayments) to patients who qualify for public assistance. If a state pays additional benefits, or if a state pays benefits to some who do not qualify for public assistance, it may require cost sharing, but payments made by patients must be small.

TRICARE

TRICARE pays benefits for health care expenses of people associated with the seven uniformed services. The uniformed services include the four branches of the military (the Army, the Navy, the Air Force, and the Marine Corps) plus the

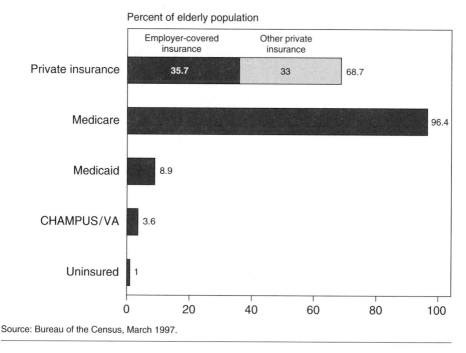

FIGURE 17.2

Sources of Health Insurance for 31.4 Million Americans 65 and Older

Percent of elderly population

Source: Bureau of the Census, March 1997.

Coast Guard, the National Oceanic and Atmospheric Administration, and the Public Health Service. Persons eligible for TRICARE include members of the uniformed services, retirees from the services, and the dependents of both. Eligibility for TRICARE ends at age 65, when covered persons become eligible for Medicare. TRICARE replaced a similar program, CHAMPUS, in 1997.

Much of the health care for people associated with the uniformed services is provided directly by the government in military hospitals and clinics. The TRICARE program is intended to pay benefits for the health care services these people receive from civilian providers.

TRICARE beneficiaries must pay deductibles and coinsurance, and insurers have developed and marketed TRICARE supplement insurance to help cover these payments.

Summary

There are several federal laws that have an important impact on health insurance.

- ERISA protects the interests of participants in employer-sponsored group health insurance plans.
- HIPAA seeks to expand the availability of health insurance.
- COBRA guarantees the continuation of health insurance coverage in some cases in which a person changes or loses her job.
- The Family and Medical Leave Act (FMLA) guarantees the continuation of employer-sponsored group health insurance benefits when a person is on family or medical leave.
- Various laws prohibit discrimination in health insurance matters on the basis of race, religion, age, sex, disability, and other such criteria.
- The Fair Credit Reporting Act regulates how health insurers can collect, use, and report personal information.

The three main federal health benefits programs are:

- Medicare for the elderly;
- Medicaid for the poor; and
- TRICARE for members and retirees of the uniformed services and their dependents.

INDEX

OTHER HEALTH INSURANCE TEXTBOOKS FROM HIAA

Study Guide for Health Insurance Nuts and Bolts

The study guide that accompanies this book makes learning easier. The study guide contains questions, exercises, and word problems that help you become familiar with concepts, procedures, and vocabulary. An answer key is included. The use of study guides is strongly recommended to those taking HIAA examinations.

The Health Insurance Primer: An Introduction to How Health Insurance Works

This book precedes *Health Insurance Nuts and Bolts* and, together with it, serves as a complete introduction to the health insurance field. The authors assume no prior knowledge and begin by explaining basic concepts and terminology, but they progress to an in-depth examination of such topics as the various kinds of health insurance, health insurance contracts, underwriting, and sales and marketing. *The Health Insurance Primer* is an excellent choice for beginners in health insurance.

Medical Expense Insurance

For those who have a basic understanding of the concepts and functioning of health insurance, this book provides more specific information on medical expense insurance, the most common kind of health insurance in America. The text begins by describing the two coverages that provide health insurance to most Americans: group major medical insurance and individual hospital-surgical insurance. Subsequent chapters discuss the following topics: marketing and sales, pricing, contract provisions, underwriting, policy administration, claims administration, and industry issues.

Managed Care: Integrating the Delivery and Financing of Health Care, Part A

An introduction to the field of managed health care. This book explains what managed care is, introduces the concepts on which it is based, and describes how it works in the real world. It presupposes no prior knowledge of either managed care or insurance. Topics include: the development of managed care; cost control techniques; measuring and improving quality; types of managed care organizations; and the involvement of government in managed care.

Managed Care: Integrating the Delivery and Financing of Health Care, Part B

Part B of HIAA's managed care series covers operational issues and problems. Topics include: governance and management structure of managed care organizations; selective medical provider contracting; network administration and provider relations; marketing and member services; claims administration; financing, budgeting, and rating; legal issues; accreditation; and regulation.

Managed Care: Integrating the Delivery and Financing of Health Care, Part C

Part C of this series examines current issues in managed care, operations and problems in specialized areas of managed care, and the role of managed care in government health care programs. Topics include: public and private purchasing groups; consumers and physicians; managed care for pharmacy, dental, behavioral health, and vision benefits; and managed care for federal employees and military personnel, in the Medicare program, and in state government programs.

Fraud: The Hidden Cost of Health Care

This book examines the problem of fraud in the health insurance industry and its investigation and prevention. Topics include: insurers' anti-fraud activities; criminal investigations and government anti-fraud efforts; investigative techniques and case preparation; automated tools for detection and investigation; fraud in managed care arrangements; fraud and electronic data interchange; legal issues; and disability income fraud.

Long-Term Care: Knowing the Risk, Paying the Price

What long-term care is, and what it is not. Who needs it, who provides it, and the traditional ways of financing it. Topics include: how consumers have reacted to the potential need for long-term care and its costs; long-term care benefits of government programs; marketing and operations; regulation; and future directions of long-term care.

Supplemental Health Insurance

This book is intended to provide those with a basic knowledge of health insurance and supplemental health insurance with more specific information on the major supplemental products in the marketplace. In addition, the gaps in health coverage that led to the need for additional insurance are discussed for each product. Topics include: Medicare supplements, hospital indemnity coverage, specified disease insurance, accident coverage, dental plans, specialty plans, and the supplemental insurance market.

THESE BOOKS MAY BE ORDERED BY CALLING 1-800-828-0111

HIAA'S SELF-STUDY COURSES AND PROFESSIONAL DESIGNATIONS

For more than 40 years, the Health Insurance Association of America's Insurance Education Program has offered current, comprehensive, and economically-priced self-study courses for professionals seeking to advance their understanding of the health insurance industry. Since 1958, more than 300,000 people have enrolled in these courses. Most enrollees are employees of health insurance companies or managed care organizations, but consultants, third-party administrators, agents, brokers, and other health insurance professionals also study with us. In addition, an increasing number of noninsurance professionals, including health care providers, economists, consumer advocates, and government officials, are taking HIAA courses to gain a better understanding of the operations of our industry and to advance their careers in their own fields.

Courses include:

- The Fundamentals of Health Insurance (Parts A and B)
- Managed Care (Parts A, B, and C)
- Medical Expense Insurance
- Supplemental Health Insurance
- Disability Income Insurance
- Long-Term Care Insurance
- Health Insurance Fraud

The completion of HIAA courses leads to two widely respected professional designations: **Health Insurance Associate (HIA)** and **Managed Healthcare Professional (MHP).** The HIA designation has been in existence since 1990 and is currently held by more than 16,500 professionals. The MHP, offered for the first time in 1996, is held by more than 4,000 designees.

For more information visit our website (www.hiaa.org) or call 800-509-4422.

HIAA INSURANCE EDUCATION PROGRAM

Gregory F. Dean JD ChU ChFC
Executive Director

Deirdre A. McKenna JD
Associate Director

Michael G. Bell
Assistant Director

Leanne Dorado
Manager of Education Operations

Kevin Gorham
Fiscal Manager

La' Creshea Makonnen
CE Credit Manager

Yolaunda Janrhett
Registration Coordinator

Matthew Grant
Internet Coordinator